Criminal Profiling

Other titles in the Crime Scene Investigations series:

Criminal Profiling

by Jenny MacKay

LUCENT BOOKS
A part of Gale, Cengage Learning

GALE
CENGAGE Learning™

Detroit • New York • San Francisco • New Haven, Conn • Waterville, Maine • London

GALE
CENGAGE Learning™

LIBRARY OF CONGRESS CATALOGING-IN-PUBLICATION DATA

MacKay, Jenny, 1978-
   Criminal profiling / by Jennifer MacKay.
      p. cm. — (Crime scene investigations)
   Includes bibliographical references and index.
   ISBN 978-1-59018-990-0 (hardcover)
 1. Criminal behavior, Prediction of—Juvenile literature. 2. Criminal profilers—
Juvenile literature. I. Title.
   HV6027.M33 2009
   363.25'8--dc22
                                                          2008021128

Lucent Books
27500 Drake Rd
Farmington Hills MI 48331

ISBN-13: 978-1-59018-990-0
ISBN-10: 1-59018-990-6

Printed in the United States of America
1 2 3 4 5 6 7 12 11 10 09 08

Contents

Foreword

The popularity of crime scene and investigative crime shows on television has come as a surprise to many who work in the field. The main surprise is the concept that crime scene analysts are the true crime solvers, when in truth, it takes dozens of people, doing many different jobs, to solve a crime. Often, the crime scene analyst's contribution is a small one. One Minnesota forensic scientist says that the public "has gotten the wrong idea. Because I work in a lab similar to the ones on *CSI*, people seem to think I'm solving crimes left and right—just me and my microscope. They don't believe me when I tell them that it's just the investigators that are solving crimes, not me."

Crime scene analysts do have an important role to play, however. Science has rapidly added a whole new dimension to gathering and assessing evidence. Modern crime labs can match a hair of a murder suspect to one found on a murder victim, for example, or recover a latent fingerprint from a threatening letter, or use a powerful microscope to match tool marks made during the wiring of an explosive device to a tool in a suspect's possession.

Probably the most exciting of the forensic scientist's tools is DNA analysis. DNA can be found in just one drop of blood, a dribble of saliva on a toothbrush, or even the residue from a fingerprint. Some DNA analysis techniques enable scientists to tell with certainty, for example, whether a drop of blood on a suspect's shirt is that of a murder victim.

While these exciting techniques are now an essential part of many investigations, they cannot solve crimes alone. "DNA doesn't come with a name and address on it," says the Minnesota forensic scientist. "It's great if you have someone in custody to match the sample to, but otherwise, it doesn't help.

That's the investigator's job. We can have all the great DNA evidence in the world, and without a suspect, it will just sit on a shelf. We've all seen cases with very little forensic evidence get solved by the resourcefulness of a detective."

While forensic specialists get the most media attention today, the work of detectives still forms the core of most criminal investigations. Their job, in many ways, has changed little over the years. Most cases are still solved through the persistence and determination of a criminal detective whose work may be anything but glamorous. Many cases require routine, even mind-numbing tasks. After the July 2005 bombings in London, for example, police officers sat in front of video players watching thousands of hours of closed-circuit television tape from security cameras throughout the city, and as a result were able to get the first images of the bombers.

The Lucent Books Crime Scene Investigations series explores the variety of ways crimes are solved. Titles cover particular crimes such as murder, specific cases such as the killing of three civil rights workers in Mississippi, or the role specialists such as medical examiners play in solving crimes. Each title in the series demonstrates the ways a crime may be solved, from the various applications of forensic science and technology to the reasoning of investigators. Sidebars examine both the limits and possibilities of the new technologies and present crime statistics, career information, and step-by-step explanations of scientific and legal processes.

The Crime Scene Investigations series strives to be both informative and realistic about how members of law enforcement—criminal investigators, forensic scientists, and others—solve crimes, for it is essential that student researchers understand that crime solving is rarely quick or easy. Many factors—from a detective's dogged pursuit of one tenuous lead to a suspect's careless mistakes to sheer luck to complex calculations computed in the lab—are all part of crime solving today.

Profiling Criminals and Their Crimes

> There's a cold-blooded scoundrel! That fellow will rise from crime to crime until he does something very bad, and ends on a gallows.
>
> —Sherlock Holmes[1]

Sherlock Holmes, although a fictional character, was one of the first and certainly the most famous detectives to use psychology in solving his cases. The mystery in the short story "A Case of Identity," bored Holmes. It involved only domestic violence, and as he said, "You will find parallel cases, if you consult my index."[2]

The very fact that Holmes kept a record of all his past cases, however, and was able to predict that the man's crimes would escalate, are marks of an experienced criminal profiler.

Sherlock Holmes, of course, "lived" in the 1800s, in the imagination of British writer Arthur Conan Doyle. The cases he solved were as imagined as he was. It would be nearly a century before criminal profiling became a standard part of solving real-life crimes.

Just the same, modern criminal profilers, the men and women who delve into the criminal mind to craft a written picture of a suspect, are often compared to Sherlock Holmes. They sift through all the details of a crime and focus just on those that point to the offender. They are the modern-day puzzle solvers of the whodunit world, collecting overlooked clues at crime scenes and from victims to create a description of the kind of person who would commit such a crime, right down to the kind of place the person might live, or the kind of car the person might drive, or even what the person might be wearing when the police come knocking on the door.

Fictional British detective Sherlock Holmes kept a record of all his past cases and was skilled in criminal and crime scene analysis, all marks of an experienced criminal profiler.

Like Sherlock Holmes, profilers usually work alone, stepping in to offer advice on a difficult case police cannot solve. They are wise detectives who have seen it all. They may be asked to lend a helping hand in cases involving a bombing, arson, bank robbery, kidnapping, a missing person, or a person held hostage. They are perhaps best known for their ability to identify the most sinister criminal of all, the serial killer.

CHAPTER 1

What Profilers Do

Solving crime is a tough job. The crime scene alone is filled with countless details that could point right to the criminal—or be overlooked. Even when all the evidence has been collected, investigators may find themselves facing a long list of seemingly useless clues: a fraction of a shoeprint, or a strand of hair that matches no DNA on file. One of the next steps is talking to potential suspects, and there might not be any. Or there might be too many. If a dead body is discovered at a shopping mall, for instance, hundreds of shoppers could be possible suspects.

Criminal investigation is always a team effort, but for certain kinds of crimes, police often turn to a criminal profiler to help them identify potential suspects.

A Day in the Life of a Profiler

In 2002 a sniper was shooting people at various locations near Interstate 95 from Maryland to Virginia. Snipers use high-powered guns that allow them to shoot from a hiding place some distance away. Unsuspecting people were getting shot and killed in parking lots and at gas stations. No one knew who the killer would target next, and the frightened public looked to law enforcement with high expectations. With every new murder, the police seemed to be failing at their job of keeping the community safe.

This is the type of case in which profilers specialize. Serious crimes, usually involving violence or murder, and serial crimes, violent crimes committed over and over by the same person or people, are where profilers are the most help. In many ways, they delve into the darkest side of crime. They are called in

for the most gruesome and brutal cases. The work of criminal profilers is often key to making an arrest.

"Criminal profiling," says Gregg O. McCrary, author of *The Unknown Darkness: Profiling the Predators Among Us*, "may be defined as 'a process used to analyze a specific crime or series of crimes in order to develop a behavioral composite of an unknown offender.'"[3] Essentially, he says, "the method and manner in which a crime is committed reflects an offender's personality traits. Thus, through an accurate assessment of those details, we can draw certain logical inferences about the offender."[4]

Inference is another word for *guess*—an educated guess, perhaps, but a guess just the same. Criminal profilers do not have supernatural powers. They do not pull the name of an offender out of thin air. What they do is give police departments a guide for where to look. They suggest what kind of person most likely committed the crime, and they might also be able to guess where and when the criminal will strike again. They do this using theories of behavioral psychology.

One of the Washington, D.C. area beltway snipers, John Allen Muhammad, is led into a Prince William County, Virginia court in 2003. Profilers specialize in violent crime cases committed over and over by the same person.

"The reason for many local agencies requesting a criminal profile is to help focus the investigation and perhaps narrow down the pool of suspects,"[5] says McCrary.

Words such as *perhaps* and *maybe* are typical in most profilers' reports. This, paired with the fact that the profiling technique is quite new compared to other crime-solving methods, such as fingerprint comparison, make many people question the value of profiling. If it does not lead to facts, some ask if it is really forensic science.

Many professional profilers say their job is a mix of science, skill, instinct, and experience. And historically, professional profilers have been accurate in the assessments they provide to law enforcement.

Such was the case in the first "modern" criminal profile, when one psychiatrist came up with a list of characteristics so similar to those of the criminal in question that it convinced the Federal Bureau of Investigation (FBI) to create a special department just for criminal profilers.

The Case of the Mad Bomber

For sixteen years during the 1940s and 1950s, a serial bomber was at work, detonating three dozen bombs in crowded, busy areas of New York City, such as Radio City Music Hall and Grand Central Station. Explosion after explosion, he slipped through investigators' hands. The bomber came to be known as the Mad Bomber, one of the most destructive criminals of the twentieth century.

Dr. James Brussel, who had studied the teachings of famed psychiatrist Sigmund Freud, believed the Mad Bomber was leaving behind more clues than the police had been able to see. While law enforcement officers sifted through physical evidence at the scenes of the bomber's handiwork, Brussel turned his attention to the bomber himself. Looking at patterns of behavior that were evident from the growing number of crime scenes, Brussel came up with a list of characteristics and traits that most likely defined the Mad Bomber. He guessed at the man's race, age, weight, and religion.

Brussel came up with details about the bomber's personality, too, and how he probably treated other people. He described a man who likely lived in one of three states—Connecticut, New Hampshire, or Maine—with one of his siblings. He even predicted how the Mad Bomber preferred to dress, going so far as to state that he would probably be wearing a buttoned, double-breasted suit when he was finally arrested. It was a long list of surprisingly specific details, and it was perhaps the first official criminal profile to be used in solving a crime.

George Metesky was finally identified by police and arrested in 1957 in Connecticut (one of the three states Brussel had named) in a home he shared with his two sisters. "When the police finally tracked down George Metesky," says McCrary, "he was in his robe, so they requested he get dressed. He came out buttoning up a double-breasted suit, just as Brussel had predicted. Most of his other details checked out as well. It was impressive."[6]

"Mad Bomber" George Metesky (foreground) behind bars in 1957. This was the first time a psychological profile was used to track down a criminal.

For perhaps the first time in history, a new crime-fighting tool had been used to track down a criminal—a psychological profile. "A psychiatrist usually studies a person and makes reasonable predictions about how that person may react to a specific situation and about what he or she may do in the future," say FBI profiler John Douglas and his coauthors in the article, "Criminal Profiling from Crime Scene Analysis." What is done in profiling "is to reverse this process. Instead, by studying an individual's deeds one deduces what kind of person the individual might be."[7]

A New Direction in the FBI

Brussel's profile convinced the FBI that psychology was a valuable tool for solving crime. In 1972 it created the Behavioral Science Unit, or BSU. At the time, the unit had only eleven

The FBI created the Behavioral Science Unit, or BSU, in 1972, which specialized in criminal profiling.

Becoming an FBI Profiler

Job Description:
FBI agents involved in the task of criminal profiling are special supervisory agents with the National Center for the Analysis of Violent Crime (NCAVC). They work with law enforcement agencies around the world to examine and review crime scene evidence, develop profiles of unknown criminals, assist with investigations, and help police and prosecutors determine the motive in a particular crime.

Education:
All FBI agents are required to have a four-year college degree and complete an eighteen-week training program at the FBI Academy in Quantico, Virginia. Agents applying for the NCAVC usually also have a master's or doctorate degree in behavioral or forensic science.

Qualifications:
An applicant must have three to ten years of experience as an FBI agent specializing in violent crimes and be recommended for the FBI's profiler training program.

Additional Information:
Positions with the NCAVC are extremely competitive. Successful candidates usually have a wealth of investigative experience in violent crime, as well as strong verbal and written communication skills. Frequent travel is a requirement of this job, and special agents typically work at least fifty hours a week.

Salary:
$60,000 to more than $150,000 per year

By the Numbers

24

Usual number of profilers employed by the FBI, eight in each of its three behavioral analysis units.

agents, and it was run from the basement of the FBI headquarters in Quantico, Virginia. Those early "official" profilers were like a new, secret weapon in solving the worst crimes being committed in America—including serial murders.

Only a handful of agents worked for the BSU in its early years—but not because there was a lack of people interested. The FBI recognized even then that not everyone is cut out for criminal profiling. The BSU painstakingly chose and personally trained its own agents, investigators with the right experience and a special knack for reading the behavior of the pathological criminals who hurt and kill again and again.

"Profiling violent crimes and their perpetrators is not an easy task," says Deborah Schurman-Kauflin in her book *The New Predator: Women Who Kill.* "Profiling begins with raw emotion because feeling is what drives serial behavior."[8]

Criminal profiling is more of a calling than just a job. Not all who claim the title of "profiler" are genuine. The true experts at this difficult form of investigation are an elite group, indeed.

Who Profilers Are

Perhaps because a certain amount of guesswork goes into every criminal profile (even expert profilers admit this), many people believe that anyone with good intuition about people could make a decent profiler. Movies and television have done much to propel this myth. But the FBI handpicks its profilers for good reason. A special combination of training and experience—lots of experience—is the recipe for a good profiler.

The right personality is a factor, too. Modern-day BSU agents no longer have to work in a basement, but the subject matter they study is no less dark. Day in and day out, they look at pictures of mangled human bodies and read gruesome

Profile of a Nazi

One of the earliest and most high-profile portraits of a deviant mind was created by psychiatrist Walter Langer for the U.S. government during World War II. Langer's assignment? Profile Adolf Hitler.

American officials wanted the scoop on the German leader. If he was captured, they wanted help on how to handle the interrogation. They wanted to know what motivated the man, and what he might do if things did not go his way.

Among Langer's profile characteristics was the prediction that Hitler would commit suicide if he was losing the war. And Langer was right. Once Germany's looming defeat was certain, Hitler killed himself.

It was the end of one criminal era and the beginning of another—profiles were on their way to being a standard step in understanding a criminal mind.

One of the earliest profiles was of Adolf Hitler.

reports of crimes so violent that most of the details are carefully kept out of the news. These are the rare investigators who can distance themselves from the very darkest side of human nature, finding valuable clues underneath all the gore.

"Investigators traditionally have learned profiling through brainstorming, intuition, and educated guesswork," say Douglas and his coauthors. "Their expertise is the result of years of accumulated wisdom, extensive experience in the field, and familiarity with a large number of cases."[9]

Specialists in profiling are either psychologists or psychiatrists who received police training to apply their knowledge of human behavior to criminal investigation, or they are police investigators who completed extra training to specialize in studying the human mind. Either way, profilers are highly educated people who have seen and studied a great deal of crime.

Profile of a Profiler

According to Schurman-Kauflin, all professional profilers have certain essential skills and knowledge. First and most important is the study of crimes: many, many crimes. Profilers are able to create accurate profiles because they have seen or read about similar crimes before. It is an occupation that depends on studying and remembering vast amounts of detail.

Qualified profilers usually have an advanced degree in criminal justice or psychological science, are trained and mentored by other expert profilers, and have firsthand experience tracking down serial criminals and talking to those who have already been caught.

"Many people make the mistake of thinking that because multiple murderers are often in the popular media that they would be easy to study," Schurman-Kauflin says. "Nothing could be further from the truth. These killers are difficult to work with, and the subject matter is dark."[10]

Unfortunately, criminal profiling is often misunderstood by the general public. Untrained "profilers" sometimes try to help during difficult cases and make the job of catching

a criminal harder for law enforcement officers and expert profilers alike.

Such was the case during the sniper killings along Interstate 95 (I-95) in Pennsylvania. People were dying, and the public demanded that police catch the killer. There was much speculation in the media about who the killer might be and what he was going to do next.

Reading a few books and watching television shows or a movie on the subject do not make a person a profiler. Not even a medical degree will do the trick. "With no behavior to assess except for accurate marksmanship, commentators shot from the hip and offered all sorts of ideas," says author and criminal justice professor Katherine Ramsland. "It soon became clear that the offender was listening to what the commentators and police were predicting, because whatever was concluded about 'him' was soon undermined."[11]

Amateur profilers stated in the news that the killer did not shoot kids—but then a kid was shot. When the news media printed and broadcast that the killer took weekends off from killing, the first weekend shooting took place.

The unprofessional profiles provided to the media by unqualified people probably led to even more shootings. They also led everyone, even police, down the wrong path. One

The Bushmaster rifle used by the Washington, D.C. area snipers is presented during their trial in 2006. Many people mistakenly believe that cases involving multiple murders are easier to solve.

profile stated that the killer, like most sniper criminals in the past, was white (he was not), that he worked alone ("he" was actually two black men working as a team), and that he drove around in a white van. Police, desperate to stop the slayings and facing pressure from the public to follow up on every lead, started looking for the wrong suspect altogether, in part because of an overload of "profiles" from people who were not expert profilers.

The killers, meanwhile, watched their fame increase on television, and it seemed they made a sport of the media attention. "One of them later admitted that he shot certain people after watching the police chief on news programs try to anticipate what he would or would not do next," says Ramsland.[12]

When the snipers were finally caught and the profiles the public had been hearing about in the news turned out to be entirely wrong, people began to have serious doubts that criminal profiling had any value at all.

Deducing, Not Inducing, a Criminal

It is true that profiling, even for experts, always requires a certain amount of guessing. There is always a chance that profilers might be wrong. The difference between what expert profilers (usually FBI agents with special training and many years of experience) provide and what the public heard during the I-95 case is the important difference between deductive and inductive reasoning.

One of the most common beliefs about criminal profiling is that it creates a recipe of a type of criminal; police merely look up a profile for a standard killer (or arsonist, or carjacker) and head out to arrest someone like that. This was one of the problems in the "profiles" created for the I-95 sniper. Working from statistics about snipers in general to reach a conclusion about that particular sniper, amateurs used inductive reasoning to paint a picture of a white shooter. Based on statistics, a mold was created of the type of person who would probably fit that crime.

FBI profiler Gregg McCrary is pictured in 2003. One problem with the profiles that are put together during a case is that they tend to include too many suspects, and can lean towards stereotyping.

McCrary says profiles based on inductive reasoning are generally "templates laid over a specific population in an attempt to predict who within that group might have an elevated potential for committing a certain type of violence." A common problem with inductive profiles, he says, "is that they become overly inclusive and dependent on stereotyping, which can result in suspicions of the wrong people while allowing actual offenders to remain free."[13]

Expert profilers, on the other hand, look at each case individually. They sift through every bit of evidence investigators have, and they look for clues about the behavior of the person who left that evidence behind. "Through this intense review process, a 'behavioral' blueprint of the crime and the offender can be constructed," says profiler Mary Ellen O'Toole. "This blueprint allows a profiler to re-create what happened at the scene."[14]

Profilers try to answer two questions: Exactly what happened, and what kind of person would do that particular thing? Thus, they practice deductive reasoning, examining the details

By the Numbers

36

Number of convicted serial killers interviewed by FBI agents in the first five years after the bureau created its Behavioral Science Unit in 1974.

of one particular crime to form a theory about what one particular criminal was thinking, what kind of person would think that way, and why. From the answers to these questions, profilers come up with possible characteristics of the criminal, based not on statistics of similar crimes but on the details of that single crime. They look at the crime as if they were the criminal, trying to understand thought processes and behavior. Deductive reasoning deals with causes and effects, not stereotypes and statistics.

Ramsland says a common error is the idea that "profiling is a sort of blueprint or set list of traits for certain criminal categories against which one can measure people to see if they might be viable suspects." But, she says, "that's the wrong question. More accurately, law enforcement interested in a profile would ask, 'From what you see at this crime scene, what traits or behaviors in a person might we be looking for?'"[15]

Both types of reasoning might come up with the same details, such as the probable age, race, and gender of the suspect or whether the person is rich or poor. But profilers reason through the crime by examining the crime scene and placing themselves in the offender's shoes. They link what was done at the crime scene to why the offender would do that, and thus, what kind of life the offender probably leads. It is always a question of behavior. Profilers ask not only what and who, but *why*.

"A basic premise of criminal profiling is that the way a person thinks … directs the person's behavior," say Douglas and his coauthors. "Thus, when the investigative profiler analyzes a crime scene and notes certain critical factors, he or she may be able to determine the motive and type of person who committed the crime."[16]

Creating a Criminal Profile

When a profiler is called in to look at a new case, there are basic steps to follow. The first step in creating a profile is to look at all of the evidence investigators collected. Profilers have no part in processing a crime scene. They do not dust for fingerprints or look for blood stains on carpets. In fact, most never visit the crime scene itself.

Instead, they pore over the evidence collected. In a murder case, they look closely at pictures of the victim that were taken at the scene. They read the autopsy report and police reports. They note every detail of the crime, down to what the weather was like that day and what meal the victim had recently eaten. There is only one detail a profiler does not want: any information on possible suspects. "Such information may subconsciously prejudice the profiler and cause him or her to prepare a profile matching the suspect,"[17] say Douglas and his coauthors.

The next step in the profiling process is to classify the crime. In a murder case, the profiler looks at the number of victims

One of the convicted I-95 snipers, Lee Boyd Malvo, enters a Virginia courtroom in 2004. Originally, working off of statistics, amateurs working the case thought that the shooter was white. Experts in the field know they need to treat each case individually to come up with a viable profile.

Hollywood Profiling: Fact or Fiction?

In 1991 the movie *The Silence of the Lambs*, starring Anthony Hopkins and Jodie Foster, was released. It seemed to shed light on the FBI's Behavioral Science Unit (BSU) and its mysterious approaches to solving crime. But just how accurate was the movie? Some experts say not very. Here are a few of the reasons why:

In the movie:
Agent Clarice Starling is still in FBI training when she joins the BSU.
In reality:
Agents newly assigned to the BSU are veterans of the FBI, usually with about ten years on the job.

In the movie:
Agent Starling personally sneaks into a storage warehouse—by herself—to look for the remains of a serial killer's victim.
In reality:
Law enforcement officers, not profilers, look for and collect evidence.

In the movie:
Agent Starling personally (and single-handedly) stops Buffalo Bill, the killer the FBI is trying to catch throughout the movie.
In reality:
Law enforcement officers, not profilers, go door to door in neighborhoods looking for clues.

and what the killer's thought process might have been. Profilers decide, based on the evidence, whether the killer knew the victim or victims, and if so, how well. They also ask whether the criminal truly meant to kill anyone. From the evidence, they reconstruct the crime itself, then profile the victim or victims. Finally, they create a profile of the killer.

An expert profiler constantly compares results with the original evidence collected from the case. "The profile must fit with the earlier reconstruction of the crime," say Douglas and his coauthors. "If there is a lack of congruence, the investigative profilers review all available data [again]."[18]

When the process is complete and the profiler feels that the profile of the killer is accurate, he or she hands it over to the police investigating the case. A finished profile may change if new evidence is discovered. A profiler always tries to make sure that everything in the profile matches all of the available clues the killer left behind.

The Profiler's Specialty

If there are suspects in a crime, police compare them to the profile. Often, though, the kinds of crimes for which criminal profiles are requested are the crimes in which investigators have few or no good suspects. Usually, they are also crimes that desperately need to be solved, and quickly. When an expert profiler from the FBI is called to the case, it usually means a violent and dangerous serial criminal is on the loose.

"The investigation of serial violent and sexual crime is complex and difficult," says profiling expert D. Kim Rossmo. "Most murders are solved because they involve intimates [someone the victim knows], and the search for the offender begins with the victim's family, friends, and acquaintances."[19] There is no such obvious relationship, however, in the kinds of crimes in which most profilers specialize. These are often called "stranger crimes," crimes with no clear motive or link between the criminal and the victim.

One crime like this is frightening enough. But when a string of seemingly connected crimes begins to take place, police quickly become desperate. The longer the criminal remains free, the more victims there will be.

This is when the phone at the FBI starts to ring, and a profiler gets on the next plane to meet with the investigators who are working on the crime.

CHAPTER 2

Profiling the Crime Scene

Many profilers compare their job to that of a doctor. Profilers and doctors do many of the same things when they receive a new case. They ask a lot of questions. They examine all the evidence, including photos, X-rays, test results, and the body itself. They might do research to better understand the case, or they might ask for a coworker's opinion. When they find a similar case to compare with and they are certain that all the clues add up, they make a diagnosis.

Profilers and doctors are both focused on solving problems. One main difference between profilers and doctors is that profilers often deal with the dead while doctors deal with the living. Both, however, face an important and stressful challenge. If they miss a clue and arrive at the wrong answer, someone could die.

The Scene of the Crime

A criminal profile usually takes the form of a report delivered to a local police department that is trying to solve a series of crimes, or sometimes just a single, but particularly difficult, case. Most profiles are a professional analysis of a crime paired with the profiler's expert opinion about what kind of person would do such a thing. "I use a formula," says FBI profiler John Douglas. "How plus Why equals Who. If we can answer the hows and whys in a crime, we generally can come up with the solution."[20]

Profilers usually are not part of the crime scene investigation itself. They are typically called in after much or all of the physical evidence at the crime scene has already been collected. This is because few local police forces have criminal profilers on staff. Instead, these professionals are usually based at the FBI

A crime scene investigator secures a crime scene. Profilers are not usually part of the original investigation of the crime scene.

headquarters in Quantico, Virginia, or at field offices around the country, and they do most of their work on the road.

Most profilers want an objective view of the crime. They like to look at all the evidence on their own, and draw their own conclusions. A suggestion made by someone else could possibly influence their own thinking about what really took place. So when profilers analyze a crime scene, they usually do much of the work on paper, examining all the evidence, photographs, and police reports.

Profilers start with the location that the crime took place. This is sometimes a challenge, because many crimes take place in multiple locations. The police usually know only one location at first—where the body was found. But this may not have been where the person was killed. It may not have been where the killer first contacted the victim, either. So a complete crime "scene" can involve many different places, such as a department store parking lot where the victim was taken, the basement where the victim was killed, the river where the victim's body was dumped, and the vehicle or vehicles that carried the victim's body in between.

"The specific location set for a given crime," says profiling expert D. Kim Rossmo, "implies something about the offender, how he or she searches for victims and the associated level of organization and mobility. Generally, the greater the organization and mobility of the offender, the greater the potential complexity (i.e., the more separate locations) of the crime location set."[21]

Deciding on the scene of a crime is even more complicated when a killer purposely tries to deceive police by staging the crime scene. Some killers try to fool police into thinking the murder might actually have taken place in one location, when it was really done somewhere else.

Fortunately, expert profilers can look at clues and usually put together what really happened. They might recognize signs, for example, that the victim was killed somewhere other than where the body was found or where the murderer tried to make police think the killing happened. Although it complicates the crime, staging also tells profilers a lot about the killer. From the way the body and the final crime scene look, a profiler can often tell police not only the type of place that was likely the scene of the murder, but in what kind of place the killer probably found his victim—a crowded parking lot, perhaps, or a deserted hiking trail. A profiler can figure all this out just by the way a killer organizes the scene.

Disorganized Crime Scenes

Profiling is based largely on the question of how well the killer plans out his or her actions. There are killers who act on impulse, exploding into violence with little or no plan on what they will do after, or even during, the event. Then there are killers who carefully plan every detail of the crime in advance, down to the steps they will take to avoid being caught. The first type of killer works very differently than the second, and the scene of the crime reflects this.

In January 1978 a brutal killer was terrorizing Sacramento, California. He broke into two different homes during a single week and killed five people, badly mutilating the bodies. The sheriff of Sacramento County told newspapers that the crimes were the most grotesque he had encountered in three decades of police work. The killer came to be known as the Sacramento Vampire because of evidence at the scenes that indicated he drank the blood of his victims.

Fortunately, two different profilers gave police detailed (and, as it turned out, extremely accurate) profiles of the killer's personality and where they would find him. The profilers' first clues came from looking at the crime scenes. They were classic disorganized crime scenes. In a disorganized crime scene, there is evidence that the crime was committed suddenly, with little or no planning. The actual killing or murder took place quickly and violently. The victim, in a disorganized crime scene, was clearly taken by surprise.

A disorganized murderer usually silences the victim quickly, because the plan is not well thought out and he fears his victim might fight back or make enough noise to draw attention to the scene. Disorganized crime scenes are usually a sign of a killer who has below-average intelligence and most likely suffers from a mental illness.

Russell Vorpagel, one of the FBI profilers who worked on the Sacramento Vampire slayings, deduced that the killer was disorganized because he shot and killed the victims before he mutilated their bodies. "This type of crime—an unorganized,

FBI agents Robert Ressler (seen here) and Russell Vorpagel developed the profile of the "Sacramento Vampire." They concluded that the killer was disorganized and possibly psychotic.

brutal, blitzkrieg attack, with no logical motive—was done by a seriously mentally disturbed person,"[22] says Joseph Harrington in his biography of Vorpagel, *Profiles in Murder: An FBI Legend Dissects Killers and Their Crimes*.

The profilers' assessments of the Sacramento Vampire's crime scenes led them to other conclusions, as well. The killer was probably white, because his victims were white and murderers usually kill people who are of their own race. Based on similarities with other crime scenes they had analyzed in the past, the profilers also suspected that the killer probably lived alone in a filthy home. And because disorganized killers usually act on impulse and tend to live within walking distance of their crimes, the profilers predicted the Sacramento Vampire's home would be within 1 mile (1.6km) of both crime scenes.

These and other details in the profiles helped police track down the killer. Once they knew they would be looking for a certain type of man who lived within a mile of the murders, the search became much easier. The profile, says Harrington, helped in a mathematical way. "It would narrow the search," he explains. "It would save time."[23] The race was on, because

Organized Versus Disorganized

Scenes of murders and other violent crimes may be organized, showing that the crime was planned, or disorganized, showing that the offender acted on impulse. Here are some of the ways profilers tell them apart:

Organized scene:
> The victim was restrained.
> The body was hidden from view or moved somewhere else.
> The murder weapon is gone.
> The offender left no physical evidence, or tried to cover it up.
> Damage to the body was done before death.

Disorganized scene:
> The victim was killed swiftly, not restrained.
> The body was left in plain sight at the scene.
> The murder weapon is still there.
> The offender was sloppy, leaving plenty of physical evidence.
> Damage to the body was done after death.

Most crime scenes are mixed—partly organized, partly disorganized. The above details are still important behavioral clues that can point profilers in a new direction.

the profilers in the case also predicted the killer would strike again soon if he was not caught.

The Sacramento Vampire, Richard Trenton Chase, was captured five days after his first murders and one day after the murders at the second crime scene. He had a history of mental illness, as the profiles had predicted. Nonetheless he eventually received the death penalty for his heinous crimes.

Profilers recognize disorganized crime scenes like those of the Sacramento Vampire in many ways. Not only is there evidence that the victim was suddenly and violently attacked, usually from behind, but disorganized crime scenes also tend to be messy. They usually involve only one location. The killer murders his victims where he finds them, and leaves the bodies at the scene.

Many profilers today believe that nineteenth-century serial killer Jack the Ripper was a disorganized criminal, and he was never caught.

There is a lot of physical evidence to be collected at a disorganized scene, including fingerprints and footprints. The killer acts impulsively, taking little or no time to cover his trail or hide what he has done. The murder weapon is often left behind at

a disorganized crime scene, too. In many cases, the weapon even comes from the scene itself, such as a knife taken from the victim's own kitchen.

It makes sense, then, that disorganized crimes are usually fairly easy to solve. "Disorganized offenders are just that: disorganized," says author Deborah Schurman-Kauflin. "Often, the more disorganized a crime scene, the more likely the individual suffers from psychosis. It follows that disorganized killers are more often one-time killers than serial offenders because they are more easily caught."[24]

Certainly, disorganized killers can and do elude police. Many modern profilers believe that the infamous, nineteenth-century London slayer Jack the Ripper was a disorganized criminal, and he was never caught. Unfortunately, violent murderers are not always caught quickly, even when the best profilers are at work on the case. Some killers go on killing sprees that last decades. Generally, this type of killer leaves behind a crime scene that shows evidence of planning down to the tiniest details, sometimes even taunting police with messages such as "Can't Catch Me." Profilers call these kinds of crime scenes "organized," and when they look at the evidence from one, they know they are probably facing a difficult case.

Organized Crime Scenes

In profiling an organized killer, a profiler notices several key factors at the scene of the murder, including planning and premeditation. There is evidence that the killer knew what he was going to do for quite a while before he did it, and that once it was done, he took steps to hide the crime, his involvement in the crime, or both. In a case of organized murder, say profilers Robert K. Ressler and Ann W. Burgess, "the crime may be committed in a secluded or isolated area selected by the murderer, or the victim may be killed in one location and transported to another." They cite a case in which the bodies of several female victims were found in various rivers, weighed down with car parts that had been tied to their bodies. "There were

Former FBI profiler Clint Van Zandt provided expert analysis to the public during the I-95 sniper shootings in Washington, D.C.

indications that they had been kept for several days before being thrown into the river. The murderer would have needed a car to transport them from where they were last seen alive to where their bodies were discovered."[25]

Crime scenes with multiple locations are considered organized. The killer took steps to cover his tracks, meaning plenty of thought went into the crime. The scenes are not impulsive and frenzied, like disorganized crimes. The killer took his time.

The primary signs of organized crime scenes, from a profiler's point of view, are evidence of planning and premeditation. Organized killers do not always try to hide evidence and avoid detection. Some of the most notorious serial murderers, in fact, do just the opposite, leaving behind deliberate clues and matching wits with the law enforcement officers who are trying to catch them.

Both kinds of offenders, however—organized and disorganized—leave trails for the detectives on the case. These are the two main ingredients of most crimes, and particularly of serial crimes. The first is modus operandi. The second, often much more sinister, is a signature.

Method of a Crime

Modus operandi, or MO for short, is a Latin term meaning the method of operating. A criminal's MO is what he does to carry out a crime to its completion. The steps involved in the MO often include things that the criminal does to avoid getting caught. An MO usually has different steps, each one aimed at helping the criminal to do three things—protect his or her identity, carry out the crime, and escape from the scene. In a robbery, a burglar's MO might include wearing gloves to avoid leaving fingerprints behind, deactivating an alarm system so it does not go off, and jumping into a stolen car to escape from the scene.

"Green River Killer" Gary Leon Ridgway, seen here in 2003, targeted prostitutes to kill, which was part of his modus operandi, or MO.

The MO of serial rapists and murderers typically includes more disturbing habits. Offenders might wear masks or disguises to protect their identity from their victims. They might prevent their victims from calling for help by gagging them or by luring them to a secluded place. They might make their escape by tying up their victims—or killing them—so they cannot get away and call the police.

An MO is important to solving cases, particularly serial crimes, because it can help police determine if different crimes were committed by the same person. Knowing the MO of criminals who have been caught can also help police find new suspects in unsolved cases or eliminate other convicted suspects who clearly have a different MO. "It is reasonable to say that all criminals have an MO, but that MO is not necessarily all that distinctive," says Brent Turvey, in his book *Criminal Profiling: An Introduction to Behavioral Evidence Analysis*. "Even when the MO in otherwise unconnected cases is precisely the same, a reasonable level of certainty has not been reached with respect to the absolute identity of the offender."[26]

In other words, says Turvey, similar MOs might only mean that two or more criminals have found that a certain way of committing a crime keeps them from getting caught. In fact, he says, criminals who spend time in prison often network with other convicts and learn even more about how to avoid getting caught when they are released from prison (many do, unfortunately, make parole and return to a life of crime).

An MO is, therefore, only one of the things a criminal profiler considers in deciding what kind of person committed a certain crime. For profilers, MOs are most useful when they reveal something specific about the criminal, something that makes him stand out from the rest. Some MOs, for instance, point to a certain skill or line of work in which the criminal may have experience. Tying up victims using a certain kind of knot could be the mark of an outdoorsman, a professional sailor, or a fisherman. Evidence that a criminal planned a perfect escape route from the building of a crime scene could help a profiler determine that police should look for a person who knows that building very well, perhaps because he lives or works there.

A criminal's MO can also change, and it often does. If a crime goes badly for him, he may learn from his mistakes and do things a bit differently the next time. It could also go the other way. A serial killer who suffers from a mental illness may begin to kill more often, and he might start to get sloppy. His MO might actually weaken over time.

Profilers often look for this kind of change in the cases they examine. The changes in MO from one serial crime to the next can tell them a great deal about the kind of person committing the crimes. Killers who get craftier are usually organized, and those who get messier are usually disorganized. But changing MOs can also make it hard to link cases committed by the same person. That is why criminal profilers also depend on another clue, one that does not change so much between crimes. This is a criminal's signature.

Manner of a Crime

Many MOs are developed for efficiency. A burglar, for example, wants to get the crime over with and get away from the scene as soon as possible. His motivation is cash or valuables. Serial killers and rapists, on the other hand, are motivated by different

Creating a Criminal Profile

Most profilers follow six general steps to help investigators track down and arrest an unknown criminal. Here is the process:

1 Examine all the evidence from the crime scene, including trace evidence, fingerprints, photographs, and police and eyewitness reports.

2 Sort through and organize the evidence, looking for patterns and similarities to other crimes and victims.

3 Reconstruct the crime scene to determine exactly what happened, where, to whom, in what order, and why.

4 Create a profile of the criminal's motives, physical qualities, personality, and other traits.

5 Give the profile to investigators in the case.

6 Interview suspects and compare them to the profile.

This bank robber was dubbed "The Mad Hatter" because he wore a different hat during each bank robbery he committed. Profilers usually find these types of signatures useful in developing an accurate picture of a criminal.

things. Many commit their crimes for the very sake of committing them. For some reason, they have a need to rape or kill. And therefore, they do certain things during their crimes, things that make the act more meaningful to them.

These things are called signatures. They are not done for the purpose of carrying out the crime, but for satisfying certain psychological or emotional needs. In fact, signatures may even hinder the crime, sometimes making it more likely that the victim will escape or that someone will catch the criminal in the act.

Profilers usually find signatures very useful in creating an accurate picture of a criminal. "A specific pattern of signature behaviors and the needs that they represent can be used to distinguish between crime scenes and potentially between offenders," says Turvey. However, "the manifestation of modus operandi behaviors and signature behaviors are not always readily apparent to even the most competent criminal profilers."[27]

Signed, The Killer

For heaven's sake catch me before I kill more. I cannot control myself.

Investigators on the trail of 1940s serial killer William Heirens found these words scribbled in lipstick on the wall of one of the murder scenes.

Heirens did not leave a lipstick note behind at all three of his brutal murders; just the same, this message was an important signature—a clue about his state of mind. Equally telling was the fact that he urinated and defecated at the scenes of his crimes. Such behaviors, unnecessary to carrying out the crime, are a profiler's favorite type of evidence. But few offenders actually take the time to "sign" their crimes in such a personality-revealing way.

Albert DeSalvo, the Boston Strangler of the 1960s, tied a bow under the chin of his victims, using socks or pantyhose, to let the police know he had struck again. Not all offenders are so considerate to investigators who are trying to link their crimes. If a criminal does have a signature, it may never be obvious unless he is caught and later admits to it.

"Lipstick Killer" William Heirens (center) is pictured in a Chicago courtroom in 1946.

Douglas gives the following example in his book, *Mindhunter*: "Take the case of a bank robber in Texas who made all of his captives undress … and took pictures of them. That's his signature. It was not necessary or helpful to the commission of the bank robbery. In fact, it kept him there longer and therefore placed him in greater jeopardy of being caught." Douglas compares this signature with that of a bank robber in Grand Rapids, Michigan, who also made everyone in the bank undress. The difference, Douglas says, was that the robber in Michigan "did it so the witnesses would be so preoccupied and embarrassed that they wouldn't be looking at him and so couldn't make a positive ID later on. This was a means toward successfully robbing the bank. This was MO."[28]

Separating an MO from a signature and linking these two elements in related crime scenes is one of a profiler's most important challenges. Failing to make these connections can lead to something profilers call linkage blindness, or the inability to draw similarities that connect one case to another and prove a serial offender is at work.

Profilers must have excellent memories for such details. Because most profilers work for the FBI, they work all over the United States, often over several decades. Some serial killers also commit their crimes in different locations around the country and sometimes even over the course of several decades. The basic signature of a serial criminal rarely changes. Remembering a signature and unique MO from one unsolved case could come in useful for the profiler when a strangely similar set of characteristics is found at the scene of another crime. Serial criminals, after all, can be mobile. Thus, as profilers evaluate crime scenes in different cities, they sometimes must compare the details to crimes in other cities.

Geographic Profiling

As the world becomes ever more mobile, so do some serial criminals. One factor profilers must consider when they examine details of a crime scene is the geography of the area where the crime occurred.

Geographic profiling is based on the idea that examining the locations and times at which a series of crimes took place can tell profilers a great deal about where the offender is likely to live and where and when he might strike again.

Research "has shown a high level of consistency in the geographic modus operandi of serial offenders, as most repeatedly employ the same crime location set," says Rossmo. "This implies that the concept of crime location could be used as an assessment for the linking of serial offenses."[29]

Considering similar locations, however, does not always mean that crimes take place in the same town, or even the same state. In fact, the more organized an offender is, the more likely he may be to change cities and throw investigators off his trail. So profilers hoping to track such a criminal across multiple states, or even countries, must look carefully at the setting of the crimes. Killers may change cities, but their crimes will often still take place in the same general locations— bodies may always be found along the side of a major highway, for example, or always in a motel room. The ability to draw connections between crimes, whether they take place across the street from one another or across the country, is one of the important talents of a profiler.

Once the crime scene has been carefully analyzed for clues and the profiler has determined what was done and how, there are still more questions to answer. Next, the profiler must learn about who was harmed or killed and determine why the killer chose this person.

CHAPTER 3

Profiling the Victim

Who becomes the victim of a crime? Most law-abiding people have asked themselves this question at one time or another. Everyone knows there are people out there who break the law, and most of us take steps to prevent becoming their victims. People lock up their homes before they go out to avoid burglary, or they may refuse to use their credit card number on the Internet or on the phone to avoid identity theft.

But what about violent crime? Who gets mugged or carjacked, raped or murdered? For a criminal profiler, studying the victim of a crime is every bit as important as studying the scene of the incident and the person who might be responsible for it. After all, the victim is always half of the crime.

Victimology

The study of crime victims, called victimology, is considered one of the most important steps in solving crimes. In violent crimes, the victim is the most important piece of evidence investigators have. The victim is the solid proof that a crime was committed. Whether the victim survived the encounter or not, the offender and the victim spent time together. Their paths crossed somehow. How these two people ended up in the same place at the same time is an important answer profilers seek when they study any violent crime.

In most cases of rape or murder, the offender and the victim knew each other. When making a list of suspects, investigators look first at family, friends, coworkers, and other people who are close to the victim. "A thorough understanding of the victim," says police officer and criminal justice instructor Michael R. King, "can often lead the investigation toward a probable suspect rather than ... to an endless pool of less likely

Stephen Grant, seen here in 2007, was convicted of murdering his wife, Tara, and dismembering her body. Although Stephen Grant made it seem like he did not know what had happened to his wife, investigators know that in most murder cases the offender and the victim know each other.

possible candidates." By examining who the victim is, King says, "we begin to unravel and eliminate an often perplexing web of misguided leads."[30]

According to the FBI's *Crime Classification Manual*, victimology generally leads to a motive, which in turn leads to suspects, and eventually, the offender. Many murder investigations are solved because a victim's circumstances show an obvious motive. A crime of fury or passion may point to an angry spouse or ex-lover. A murder victim who recently took out a large life insurance policy inevitably leads police to look first at the person who would collect all that money.

The cases that profilers take on, however, are the ones with no clear motive and no easy answers. Often, they are the cases with evidence, based on modus operandi and signature, that a serial criminal is at work. "While it is not completely accurate to say that these crimes are motiveless," say Douglas and his coauthors, "the motive may all too often be one understood only by the perpetrator."[31]

Serial crimes are not one-time offenses for revenge or money. The offender is hunting people. A criminal profiler uses victimology to determine who falls into the hunter's sights, why, and what this says about the hunter.

Random Victims

What makes some serial criminals hard to catch—and especially terrifying—is that they seem to find victims at random. Police face a difficult challenge in the race to find out how the offender works and who might be targeted next.

A bullet hole marks the spot where a random victim, Sarah Ramos, was killed by the I-95 snipers in 2002. Criminals that target random victims are more difficult to catch.

An investigator's job might be easier if a killer was murdering one employee of a particular department store every Saturday evening. Aside from just staking out the parking lot on Saturday nights, it would be easy to deduce that the killer must be someone who knows the employees of the store because he spends a lot of time there. The initial list of suspects would rapidly shrink down to include the store's employees and regular customers—a manageable load for investigators.

Far more difficult to catch is the serial offender whose victims show no such relationship to one another, who did not work in the same place, or even have a reason to know one another (or the offender). In these cases, profilers must make educated guesses about why the offender chose these particular victims. The process begins by deciding to what degree each victim put himself or herself at risk for a violent crime.

Who Is at Risk?

People who live safely and rarely venture into dangerous situations are considered by profilers to have a low risk of becoming victims of violent crime. A murdered stay-at-home mom who had young children, lived in a safe neighborhood in a home with an alarm system, and rarely went out alone after dark would be considered a low-risk victim.

A victim classified as medium risk would have had a slightly more dangerous lifestyle. This might be someone who worked the evening shift at a bar or a convenience store, lived alone in an apartment in a dangerous part of town, or preferred to walk to the store for groceries after work at ten o'clock at night.

High-risk victims are people whose lifestyle frequently would have put them in harm's way. They may have had a drug habit, and thus, spent a lot of time with dealers and other

Prescriptions for Crime

A profile does not point to specific suspects by name. Its purpose is to help police identify the type of person who might have committed the crime. Criminal profiles "diagnose" symptoms of crimes and criminals. They can help police to:

- Create a list of possible suspects.
- Narrow down a suspect list.
- Question suspects and witnesses.
- Tail suspects during undercover investigations.
- Flush suspects out of hiding, using the media and other techniques such as staking out sites the suspect is predicted to want to visit.
- Identify potential future offenders in the hope of preventing crime.

In cases of serial crime, a profile might also predict what kind of person the offender will target next, as well as where and how that victim might be targeted.

criminals. Prostitutes, because of their working hours and locations, are always at high risk for crime. However, so is a college student with no car and no money who accepts a ride from a stranger to make it home for Thanksgiving.

Profilers always try to determine the risk level of a particular victim. It has nothing to do with passing judgment on a victim and everything to do with deciding what kind of criminal is at work and how he is selecting his prey.

"The more that is known about the victim, the greater the insight investigators will have about the offender,"[32] says profiler Mary Ellen O'Toole. Cases that involve low-risk victims are easier to profile because these victims are more likely to have been targeted for crime by someone they knew, or by someone they had met before.

On the other hand, O'Toole says, "Crimes involving high-risk victims are extremely difficult to profile because these could be victimized by any number of people."[33]

Victim Characteristics: The Search for Patterns

In the late 1990s in Queensland, Australia, a serial rapist was breaking into homes in the middle of the night and attacking the women who lived there. As the tally of victims rose, police quickly saw a pattern. The rapist was choosing elderly women who lived alone and were not likely to have any visitors after midnight who might interfere with the rape.

When Queensland police took a closer look at the characteristics of the crime victims, they discovered another link between them. All of these elderly women lived in homes rented from the Queensland Housing Commission. Police quickly concluded that the rapist had chosen each of his victims ahead of time, probably because he had met them while doing something related to a job he had with the housing commission. Police predicted the offender would turn out to be a maintenance person, gardener, painter, or builder. And because, in each case, he seemed to know how the inside of the victim's home was laid out, investigators deduced that his job required him to go into people's residences.

The rapist also wore a mask and gloves during his attacks, and his victims reported that he always spoke in a whisper. From this behavior, investigators concluded the man was trying to hide his identity, probably because he had met each of the women before and he feared they might recognize him.

When the rapist was caught, it turned out that he did work for the housing commission. He was a painter and had been in each victim's home before returning in the middle of the night to rape her.

By understanding how and why the victims were chosen in this case, says author Brent Turvey, "a 'relationship' between the offender and victims was established." Other possible

Becoming a Forensic Psychologist

Job Description:
A forensic psychologist evaluates convicted criminals and trial defendants to determine their degree of sanity at the time of the crime, as well as whether they are fit to stand trial. This professional often testifies in court and sometimes helps prepare profiles of criminal offenders.

Education:
Most forensic psychologists have a master's or doctorate degree in psychology, plus additional training in the specialty of forensic psychology.

Qualifications:
Forensic psychologists hold a license to practice psychology in their state and must pass a state certification exam for forensic psychology. One year of field work in criminal justice is a bonus. Many forensic psychologists are also certified by the American Board of Forensic Psychology.

Additional Information:
Forensic psychologists can specialize in many different areas. They may work for prisons, psychiatric hospitals, law enforcement agencies, juvenile detention centers, or private consulting firms. Excellent people skills and communication skills are essential in this job.

Salary:
$40,000 to $80,000 per year

relationships include between work colleagues, neighbors, hobbyists in the same clubs, or customers who go to the same bars. "The number of possible links is endless, so a good victimology is essential to narrow this down."[34]

David Berkowitz, the "Son of Sam" killer who terrorized New York between 1976 and 1977, had a pattern of choosing young couples alone in cars or on the street as his victims. Understanding how or why victims are chosen helps investigators establish a relationship between the criminal and victim.

Profilers ask many questions about victims because, in serial crimes, the type of person that catches a criminal's attention can be a huge clue to the type of offender the criminal is. Profilers want to know all they can about victims in a case, because patterns in the way the victims look, where they live, or where they work might be clues about whom the offender will go after the next time.

In murder cases, profilers also want to know where the victims were last seen alive, where the bodies were found, and whether either location is where the murders actually took place.

"It is necessary to determine what the last known location of the victim was," says King. "Did the victim end up in that particular location because the predator chose it? Or is it a place where the victim stayed in regular circumstances?"[35]

These details are clues not only to a killer's strategy for finding victims but also to the type of offender the killer is: organized or disorganized.

Victims of Opportunity, Victims of Deceit

In the nineteenth century Jack the Ripper's victims were high-risk women—prostitutes with drinking problems who were probably not sober at the time of their death. He murdered them on the streets of London where he found them, and made little or no effort to move or hide their bodies when he was done.

Modern profilers would have seen some classic signs of a disorganized killer in Jack the Ripper. Based on the state of his victims, he killed with sudden violence, mutilated the bodies of his victims *after* they were dead, and left their bodies in plain view at the death scene—all symptoms of a killer with a disorganized personality.

A very different scene is one in which the victim is discovered in a place far from where he or she was last seen, a place where that person would not normally have spent time. These details point to a more organized offender who planned the abduction. When a victim's body is found in an unexpected place—a dead woman, for instance, found in a forest in the middle of winter wearing nothing but a thin sweater for warmth—it suggests that the killer found the victim somewhere other than where he eventually left the body. This kind of killer does not ambush his victims right where they live or work, like Jack the Ripper did; instead, he may try to trick his targets into going somewhere with him. Profilers might be looking for a much more cunning killer, one whose victims will not be limited to high-risk people such as drunken prostitutes but will include anyone he is able to trick.

Ted Bundy, who is believed to have murdered at least forty people in the 1970s, was just such a trickster. A particularly organized offender who left almost no physical evidence behind on his deadly trail across several states, Bundy captured some of his victims by luring them close with an act that he was disabled and needed help. He then turned on them violently when they got near. Profilers carefully study the victims of a killer like Bundy, trying to determine just what these women would have been likely to believe and how probable it is that they would, for instance, climb into a killer's car.

Only then does a profiler know what law enforcement officers are up against, and just how organized, persuasive, and clever the serial criminal is. "The degree of organization or disorganization can provide tremendous insights into the level of sophistication of the offender," says O'Toole, "including the approach used in accessing the victim, the style of attack, the relationship of the victim to the offender, and the type of interaction that likely took place at the scene between the offender and the victim."[36]

Stranger or Acquaintance?

Perhaps the most frightening thing about serial criminals is that in almost all cases, there will be more victims unless the person is caught and stopped. Whether these victims will be strangers to the criminal or people that he has a reason to know is an important detail. It helps determine the method he will use to find his next victim, but it also points to the kind of fantasies that are going on in the criminal's head.

Serial killer Ted Bundy participates in a prison interview just before his execution in 1989. Bundy captured some of his victims by pretending to be disabled and in need of help.

Mr. Victim

In most cases of serial murder, the victims whom profilers study are women. But in 1990 several male murder victims turned up unclothed on the side of a road, and the victimology pointed to a serial killer few investigators had seen before or since: a female lust murderer.

Killer Aileen Wuornos murdered seven men before she was captured. Unlike most sexually motivated serial killers who are males victimizing women, she was a rare example of a woman who victimized men. After shooting her victims, she removed their clothing and left them out in the open to show her contempt for the male gender.

Wuornos's criminal career was portrayed by actress Charlize Theron in the movie *Monster*.

To an experienced profiler with a good understanding of criminal psychology, whether an offender seeks out total strangers or acquaintances will point to important details about the offender himself.

Most serial killers and rapists live in an elaborate fantasy world. When the appearance or attitude of the other person in those fantasies is important to him, he usually spends time targeting the exact kind of victim who will best fit the role.

Another offender might have fantasies about situations, not about people. For this criminal, how and where he finds his victims are usually more important to his fantasy than are the victims themselves.

"A prior relationship between the victim and the offender therefore need not, and typically does not, exist," says Richard N. Kocsis, author of *Criminal Profiling: Principles and Practice*. "What is important is the role that the victim plays in the offender's fantasy."[37]

Victims of the same offender, however, will often have similarities in appearance, personality, or other characteristics, and from this, profilers may be able to determine the kind of victims at risk of being the offender's next target.

For some offenders, a victim's characteristics, or even gender, are not the important feature of the fantasy. Instead, an offender may be obsessed with situations. He may be motivated by the thrill of the chase and the excitement of almost getting caught in the act. This kind of offender may purposefully target low-risk victims in high-risk situations, caring less that his victim is an attractive blonde woman, for example, than the fact that he kidnapped her from a busy mall parking lot in broad daylight.

O'Toole says that understanding the risk level of both the victim and the offender is important to profiling a case: "How much risk did the offender take in committing this crime? Two possible explanations are that 1) the offender targeted that particular victim, or 2) this offender needed an element of high risk/high thrill in the crime to be emotionally or psychologically satisfied. Either conclusion reached by the profiler can be extremely helpful to investigators."[38]

Whether a profiler determines that a victim was targeted or was simply at the wrong place at the wrong time, getting to know the victims of a case can lead to important predictions about the offender—details that, when shared with the public, might help potential victims protect themselves.

Linking Victims

Carefully investigating the victims of violent crimes not only allows a profiler to determine a great deal about the perpetrator, but it can also help them determine whether the crimes were committed by a serial offender.

When the Boston Strangler raped and choked to death more than thirty women, mostly elderly, in their Massachusetts homes in the 1960s, he left a calling card behind, pantyhose or another piece of clothing tied in a bow under his victim's chin. Police quickly knew they had a serial killer to catch.

Not all criminals work in such obvious ways. Carefully examining the background of murder victims is the only way to reveal hidden clues that link victims no one thought were related, thus exposing the work of a sneakier serial killer.

Such was the case among the victims of a 1950s serial rapist and killer named Harvey Glatman. Other than the fact that he dumped them in the desert landscape surrounding Los Angeles, Glatman's victims had no obvious relationship to one another. But, it turned out, most of the victims had either needed cash or were interested in modeling careers at the time of their death. Glatman met them by responding to their personal ads in the newspaper and by posting ads of his own, posing as a legitimate magazine photographer.

Although a killer's victims may not look alike, live in the same neighborhood, or share other obvious features, an investigation that includes interviews with their family and friends might reveal an important link between seemingly unrelated murders—such as a shared interest in modeling, like Glatman's victims. It might also reveal the motivation of the killer and his method of finding victims.

What a profiler knows about the victims of a serial offender can also suggest ways for citizens to protect themselves. If the offender seems to be targeting college women who walk home from campus after dark, for example, the community can be warned of this danger, and students can be advised to take a shuttle or get a ride from a friend instead of walking at night. Unfortunately it is not always possible to protect oneself from danger.

When violent murderer Peter Kurten was captured in Germany after a string of grisly murders in the 1920s, he stated at his trial, "I did not kill either people I hated, or people I loved. I killed whoever crossed my path at the moment my urge

> ## By the Numbers
>
> # 3 TO 4
>
> **Number of victims a killer must have, with a cooling-off period in between, for profilers to name him or her as a serial killer.**

People originally believed that Albert DeSalvo was responsible for the "Boston Strangler" murders that occurred between 1962 and 1964. Today, some investigators think that the murders were committed by more than one person.

for murder took hold of me."[39] Kurten's statement about what motivated him to kill shows just how frightening, unpredictable, and hard to catch such a person can be.

For profilers, though, there is always a link to be found between victim and killer. After all, in one way or another, the two spent time together. An investigation into the background of a victim will somehow tie in to the identity of the offender, if the profiler is clever enough to find the connection.

CHAPTER 4

Profiling the Offender

Once all the available evidence has been collected, and the crime scene and victim have been studied in detail, a criminal profiler moves to the next step of the profiling process: making educated guesses about the type of person who committed the crime.

This is where art and science come together. Most criminal profilers claim that their job takes a little of both. There are facts to research and a scientific process to follow, but the task of actually making a claim about the characteristics, background, and personality of an unknown criminal is, by its very nature, taking a guess.

"It is important to expect that a significant number of mistakes will occur with profiling," say Robert J. Hormant and Daniel B. Kennedy in their article "Psychological Aspects of Crime Scene Profiling." Even though profiles may not be perfect, however, Hormant and Kennedy say they are certainly worthwhile: "No method that has promise should be withheld from the types of cases with which profilers typically deal."[40]

Just what type of cases *do* profilers typically handle? The reason a certain amount of guessing is allowed is because the case files sitting on a criminal profiler's desk usually represent especially gruesome and difficult-to-solve cases. A profiler's cases are usually serial crimes committed by people with some sort of mental or psychological imbalance. They are crimes that the police suspect will happen again and will probably be worse when they do.

Profilers spend their careers getting into the heads of these kinds of criminals. They interview convicts. They read arrest files. They help with police interrogations. They testify in court.

Day in and day out, they try to put themselves into the minds and bodies of serial criminals. When one is on the loose, profilers look at the facts of the case and begin to see the person, feel the person, and some say, even *be* the person. Then they create a profile.

Deductive Profiling

Profiling a criminal begins first with the facts: what was done, where, how, and to whom. Profilers want every bit of evidence police have in a case, because at first, their profession demands that they assume nothing. Instead, they use the facts to reconstruct the crime scene and narrow down exactly what happened.

This is an example of deductive reasoning, looking at known facts to conclude what the criminal has done. Deductive reasoning is essential to the profiling process because it helps answer the question of *why* the criminal

John E. List (left) is shown in this family photo with his wife and children. List became the subject of an 18-year manhunt after killing his wife, children, and mother in 1971. One aspect of the profiling process is making educated guesses about the type of person who committed the crime.

59

Criminal Versus Racial Profiling

A criminal profile is a set of personal and behavioral characteristics designed to help police identify an unknown suspect for a particular crime or predict what kind of person may commit a crime in the future.

When a criminal profile includes details about race, ethnicity, nationality, or religion, however, it may be criticized as being a racial profile.

Racial profiling is a very controversial topic in law enforcement. Reports of traffic stops and police arrests in cities across the United States, for instance, show that minority citizens are far more likely than whites to be questioned by police for a variety of offenses.

There is a difference, however, between criminal profiling and racial profiling. Racial profiles make generalizations about typical groups of people who are likely to commit a certain kind of crime.

A criminal profile, on the other hand, identifies likely characteristics of the *one* individual who committed a single, specific crime.

Whether it is fair to predict race in a criminal profile is a matter of debate. Many people think any detail that helps police find and stop a violent criminal is important. Yet, this same issue prevents most profiles from being used as evidence in a criminal trial.

did this thing, in this way, in this place, on this day, and to this person. Deductive reasoning, or gathering the facts in the case, leads a profiler to an offender's motive—what drove him or her to commit a certain crime. Was it revenge? Was it for profit?

When the profiler has seen all the available evidence in a case and has deduced what the offender did, the modus operandi (how the crime was committed), and the motive (why the crime was committed), it is time to make some educated guesses about the offender himself.

Inductive Profiling

Deducing what happened is part of any criminal investigation and any profile, and it involves the advice of many different experts, everyone from blood spatter specialists to the local authority on explosives. But inductive reasoning, or making educated guesses about what kind of person the offender is, is the specialty of the criminal profiler.

Inductive reasoning is based on research and experience. Profilers make their living studying different kinds of crimes, and more importantly, the different kinds of people who commit them. This background is critical to pinpointing the specific facts in a case that reflect the offender's behavior and important personal traits.

Much of profiling is based on recognizing patterns. A good profiler looks at all the facts of a particular case to decide

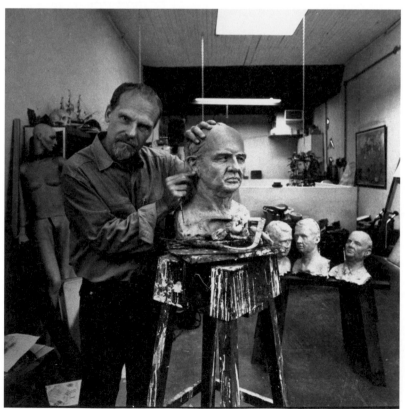

Forensic sculptor Frank Bender with his bust of mass murderer John List. The bust, created with the help of criminal psychologist Richard Walter, was shown on the television show **America's Most Wanted** *and led to List's arrest in 1989. Using deductive and inductive reasoning allows a profiler to paint a detailed picture of a criminal.*

61

Reconstructing a Crime Scene

Before deciding what type of person committed a crime and why, profilers must determine what was done and how. To answer these questions, they follow this process for reconstructing the crime:

1 Review every piece of evidence that has been collected. If any important clue is overlooked, the puzzle cannot be put back together properly.

2 Evaluate the evidence. Not all evidence is useful. An eyewitness report, for instance, can be misleading.

3 Form a hypothesis, or an educated guess, about what happened at the scene.

4 Revisit the clues. Does all the evidence support the hypothesis? If some clues do not fit, start over.

5 Test the hypothesis. Would the crime, if it were acted out again, leave the same exact evidence at the scene? If the answer is yes, the crime has been reconstructed.

6 Create the criminal profile.

which characteristics of that case likely point to characteristics of the person who committed the crime. These guesses are based partly on the details of similar crimes that have been committed in the past and partly on knowledge of human behavior. Using their vast knowledge about previous cases and about how criminals think, profilers induce, or guess, what kind of person would do the things that were done at a particular crime scene.

Inductive reasoning includes the use of statistics: If most serial killers are between the ages of twenty-five and thirty-five, for example, then a profiler would consider this probability in deciding the age of a particular killer in question.

If professional profilers used only inductive reasoning, however, anyone with a computer and access to crime databases could be a profiler. Profiling, however, is much more complicated than simply looking at statistics.

For one thing, says author Brent Turvey, inductive reasoning "is not specifically related to any one case, therefore it is not by its nature intended for reconstructing a 'profile' of an individual person."[41] He says that although profilers do depend on statistics from past cases to a certain extent, these general facts are no replacement for the skills, experience, and instinct a profiler can bring to each individual, unsolved case.

As an experienced criminal profiler works, Turvey says, "offender emotions during the offense, individual patterns of offense behavior, and offender personality characteristics are deduced from that particular offender's crime scene behavior and victimology only."[42]

Based on this blend of deductive and inductive reasoning and supported by a solid career of experience, a criminal profiler paints a detailed picture of the perpetrator who committed a specific crime.

By the Numbers

80 TO 95

The below-average IQ (intelligence quotient) among disorganized killers, often a detail predicted in profiles.

Disorganized Offenders

Just as crime scenes are classified as unorganized or well organized, so are the offenders who leave these kinds of scenes behind. In crimes of serial rape and murder, which make up the bulk of most profilers' caseloads, deciding whether the offender is organized or not allows a profiler to make other very important predictions—everything from where an offender lives and works to what kind of vehicle he drives and what kind of student he may have been in school.

"The criminal-profile-generating process is defined as a technique for identifying the major personality and behavioral characteristics of an individual based on an analysis of the crimes he or she has committed," say profiler John E. Douglas and his coauthors. "Included in the criminal profile are background information (demographics), physical characteristics, habits, beliefs and values, preoffense behavior leading to the crime, and postoffense behavior."[43]

Disorganized criminals tend to leave behind messy crime scenes with a lot of physical evidence. From this, profilers deduce that the criminal acted on the spur of the moment. Little planning went into the crime, and the offender did little to clean up after himself, leaving fingerprints, footprints, the assault weapon, and other kinds of evidence out in the open.

From the details of a disorganized crime scene, profilers may suspect certain details about the offender. Statistically,

Disorganized criminals tend to leave a lot of physical evidence at the crime scene, including fingerprints, footprints, or even the weapon used in committing the crime.

he is likely to have below-average intelligence and poor social skills and is the
youngest of his siblings.

A profiler would combine details like
these with features of the crime scene to
give police investigators a far more useful
description of the person they should be
looking for.

When a young woman named Betty
Jane Shade was killed in Pennsylvania in
1979 and her body dumped at an illegal
trash site, Douglas, the profiler on the case,
recognized clear signs of a disorganized offender and gave police
some information that helped them narrow down their suspects.

By the Numbers

400

Approximate number of serial killers who have operated in the United States during the past century.

"I thought they should be looking for a white male, aged seventeen to twenty-five," Douglas says. "He would be thin or wiry,
a loner, not exactly a whiz kid in high school." Douglas also gave
details about the killer's probable personality, home life, and type
of job. "I told the police not to look for the 'used-car salesman type
down the street with the outgoing personality.' Anyone who would
leave the body at that sort of dump site had to have a menial job
or something that involved dirt or grime."[44]

Ultimately, it turned out that there were two killers, not
one. But they were brothers, both from the kind of family
background Douglas had predicted, and they worked as trash
haulers, the kind of job he also predicted. They also fit the age
group and personality type of the profile, more so than the
other suspects police had in mind. The brothers were arrested
and convicted of Shade's murder in a case that showed how the
profile of a disorganized offender, even when slightly off target,
can put murderers behind bars before they strike again.

Organized Offenders

Organized criminals leave behind different kinds of crime
scenes, ones that show a good deal of planning and point
to an offender who is both intelligent and socially skilled.

Two British police detectives question a young man in search of serial murderer and rapist John Duffy in 1986. This case was the first in Britain to use criminal profiling and resulted in the conviction of Duffy.

When profilers see organized crime scenes, they recognize an offender who targets his victims and covers his tracks. Inductive reasoning tells them they may be dealing with someone who lives an otherwise normal life and might even be married and have a family. It is likely that the person not only will commit more crimes, but will also get better at not getting caught.

"The organized offender often uses a ruse or a con to gain control over his victim," says Robert K. Ressler, a retired FBI profiler. "This is a man who has good verbal skills and a high degree of intelligence, enough to lure the victim into a vulnerable area."[45]

Because organized offenders plan their crimes, Ressler says, the offender spends time figuring out how to trick his victims. "With the organized killer," he explains, "the offender has enough verbal and other interchange with the victims to recognize them as individuals before killing them."[46] This type of information often helps profilers create a picture of an intelligent person who acts friendly and then snares his victims.

When a criminal, later named the Railway Killer, began committing rapes near railroad tracks in London, England, in 1982, his early victims described a man whose friendly conversation had put them off guard long enough for him to attack. Then he threatened them with a knife while committing the rape.

In 1985 the rapist escalated to murder, strangling one of his victims. He went on to murder others, and the frustrated London police asked a behavioral science professor, David Canter, to create a psychological profile of the killer.

"Combining statistical analysis of witness and victim statements with his vast insight into the vagaries of human nature," says author Colin Evans in *The Casebook of Forensic Detection*, "Canter drew up a profile of the Railway Killer that suggested that he lived in the Kilburn area of northwest London, was married and childless, had a history of violence, was plagued by domestic discord, and probably had two close male friends."[47] When police compared the details of Canter's profile to their huge group of suspects, the list was quickly narrowed down from 1,999 suspects to one: John Duffy.

"Canter's profile proved accurate in thirteen of its seventeen points," says Evans. "Particularly perceptive was his suggestion that the killer was childless; this had, apparently, been a great source of anguish to Duffy."[48]

Before the profile, the Railway Killer had been impossible for the police to positively identify and track down. The case served as England's first good example of using criminal profiling to capture what may be the most dangerous human predator on Earth: the sexually motivated, organized serial killer.

Profile of an Arsonist

No good criminal profile depends on statistics alone, but whenever police track down an arsonist, they find that the criminal usually fits many points of the following profile:

Age:	teens or twenties
Gender:	male
Race:	white
Social status:	lower class or working class
IQ:	lower than normal
Home life:	abusive
School life:	learning problems; was probably held back a grade
Drug/alcohol use:	none
Criminal record:	previous arrests

Profiles in Smoke

Putting serial killers like Duffy behind bars is one of the great rewards of profiling, but not all profiled offenders are rapists or lust murderers. A profiler's skills may be put to use in solving any kind of criminal puzzle.

Serial arsonists and bombers work much differently than a lie-in-wait, organized serial rapist or a violent, disorganized murderer. A person who sets fires may not even mean to hurt anyone, although the crimes may indeed lead to deaths if fires are set in buildings where people live or work. A serial bomber, who does intend to kill, may commit his crimes from a considerable distance, and unlike other kinds of killers, may never actually see the faces of the victims at all.

Although they work differently than the rapists and murderers who make up many of a profiler's cases, arsonists and bombers usually also have some sort of psychological imbalance, and this makes them prime targets for a profiler's skills. Reading the behavioral clues of these criminals' actions, profilers may be able to point police in the exact direction of the arsonist or bomber they seek.

Profiling the Unabomber

For three decades, beginning in the 1970s, a serial bomber terrorized U.S. citizens by mailing explosives to people. During his reign as one of America's most notorious criminals, this serial bomber targeted mostly university professors and was therefore called the Unabomber. Before he was finally caught in 1996, he had killed several people and seriously injured more than a dozen others.

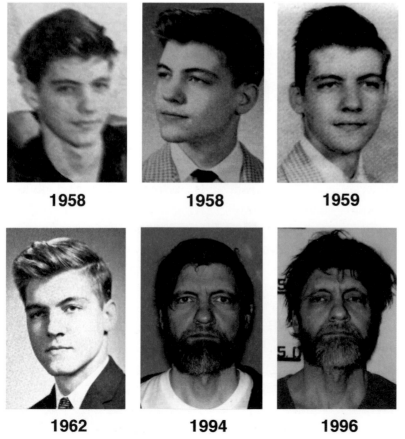

1958   1958   1959

1962   1994   1996

The many faces of the "Unabomber," Theodore Kaczynski. Kaczynski exhibited many of the traits that profilers predicted.

To help catch the criminal at the heart of what was, at the time, the most expensive criminal investigation in U.S. history, the FBI sent profilers to work on the case. In 1993 the *New York Times* printed the details of the FBI's profile. Reporter Stephen Labaton wrote that federal investigators believed the bomber was "an obsessive-compulsive white man who was reared in the Chicago area and probably has had menial jobs." The bomber, profilers predicted, was the type to visit the scene of his crimes to watch the parcel blow up. "To re-live the experience," Labaton wrote, "he probably keeps souvenirs like newspaper clippings and videotapes."[49]

When investigators finally tracked the Unabomber down, the man behind the nickname—Ted Kaczynski—did indeed fit many details of the profile. He was born in Chicago. He was in his thirties when the bombings began. And when his small Montana cabin was examined for evidence after his capture, police found it packed from floor to ceiling with "souvenirs" collected during half a lifetime of bombings.

Ultimately, the FBI's criminal profile was not the piece of the investigation that led to the Unabomber's capture. Douglas claims that by the time the profile was created, Kaczynski was already well into his criminal career and had become much more skilled at getting away.

"Most of these guys are catchable early in their careers," Douglas says, "before they start perfecting what they do and moving around the country." Having worked on the Unabomber profile himself, Douglas claims that "had we been where we are now with profiling in 1979, Unabomber might have been caught years earlier."[50]

Arson Cases

Arsonists, much like bombers, usually leave a pattern of behavior behind that a profiler can use to identify who they are.

In 2005 fifty-year-old, fast-food manager Thomas A. Sweatt was arrested for setting fire to forty-six homes and apartments in the Washington, D.C., area. The psychological

Arsonists also exhibit patterns of behavior that profilers can use to identify them. Thomas A. Sweatt was arrested for setting multiple fires in the Washington, D.C., area.

profile created to help find him determined, from the arsonist's tactic of leaving gasoline-filled jugs on front porches and lighting them with wicks so that he would have about twenty minutes to sneak away, that he was someone with a chameleon-like personality, someone who would seem to his coworkers and neighbors like a very nice person.

"He doesn't seem like the type," one of Sweatt's neighbors told the *Washington Post* after the arsonist's arrest. The neighbor said that Sweatt, true to the profiler's predictions, "kept to himself and was a nice guy."[51]

Arsonists, like other serial criminals, usually have a signature behavior and a consistent MO, making them prime candidates for criminal profiling.

"What intrigues us most about arson, especially serial arson or pyromania," says Mary Mavromatis, author of "Serial Arson: Repetitive Firesetting and Pyromania," "is that it is a crime least associated with violence and most associated with serious psychopathology."[52]

In fact, arson may even be a future serial killer's introduction to crime. Murderer David Berkowitz, whose killing spree of teenagers in the 1970s earned him the nickname Son of Sam, confessed that he had started more than two thousand fires in New York City in the years before he escalated to murder.

A history of setting fires, like a history of torturing animals, signals to profilers that a person may be gearing up for a life of the worst kinds of crimes. This is why many profilers predict details of an offender's childhood when they create a profile of a serial criminal.

Some of the cases in which childhood plays a particularly important role to the profile are those in which the predicted killer does not fit the typical profile of a serial murderer: instead of being a man aged twenty-five to thirty-five, she is a woman.

Fatal Females

Think of notorious killers and some familiar names come up: Jack the Ripper, the Zodiac Killer, Ted Bundy, and Jeffrey Dahmer. All are men.

In fact, the vast majority of serial killers are men. For this reason, criminal profilers on the hunt for deadly killers typically predict the offenders are male.

But there *are* female serial killers. They just tend to perform their crimes in different ways. Rarely are their deeds violent—at least, not in a bloody sense. They almost never torture their victims or mutilate the bodies the way many male killers do. Instead, women killers usually hide their crimes by choosing people who are very sick or very old, helpless victims whose death will not come as much of a surprise to others. The usual murder weapons of female serial killers are not knives or guns, but bottles and pillows. They prefer to poison their victims or smother them to death, choosing a modus operandi that leaves little or no evidence behind. Especially when they have jobs as caretakers of helpless persons, these criminals can remain in one place, killing quite often, and not be suspected of murder because their victims are people who were expected to die soon of natural causes, so no one realizes that the cause of death was actually homicide.

Serial killer Aileen Wuornos leaves court in Ocala, Florida in 2001. Women are much less likely to become serial killers than men, and almost never torture or mutilate the bodies of their victims the way many men do.

"There are no marks or other types of evidence to examine, making detection quite difficult," says author Deborah Schurman-Kauflin. "The pattern seems to be: many deaths surrounding one lone female caregiver."[53]

The process of profiling a female serial killer is different than profiling a male. This is because female killers are typically quite easy to catch—once someone catches on to them. They most likely live or work in the very place, even the very building, where they commit most of their murders. The challenge is figuring out that the deaths (in a nursing home, for example) were not of natural causes. Once this is determined, the suspect list will probably be small, and one caregiver will stand out among the rest as the person with a connection to all of the deaths.

Schurman-Kauflin says female killers tend to be high-school dropouts who are younger than thirty. They are usually people who played alone as children because they never fit in. Female serial killers often have a history of acne and weight problems, especially when they were teenagers, and they are often fascinated by death and torture.

Creating a profile of characteristics like these can help the investigation, even when police have a suspect. "A good profiler can construct an effective investigative and interview strategy," says Schurman-Kauflin. "The aforementioned characteristics may help narrow a field of suspects and provide insight into a killer's mind. This is what profiling is all about."[54]

One of the most infamous female serial killers in modern times was Genene Jones, a nurse in San Antonio, Texas, who is suspected of killing dozens of infants by injecting them with drugs that caused heart attacks and breathing problems. Her motive? She enjoyed the thrill of helping during the "Code Blue" emergencies as hospital staff members desperately tried to revive the babies, many of whom died despite their efforts.

"In order to estimate why an offender engages in certain behaviors," says Schurman-Kauflin, "there must be an understanding of what emotional state dominates the individual who commits the crime."[55]

Experts believe that Jones's actions may have resulted in the deaths of more than thirty children. In 1984 she was sentenced to 160 years in prison for her string of horrific crimes. She is proof that the terrifying cases demanding the expertise of a criminal profiler can take countless different forms, but they all depend on a profiler's ability to read crimes of all kinds—and the people who commit them.

CHAPTER 5

Criminal Communication in Profiling

German murderer Peter Kurten, who said in court that he killed whoever crossed his path when the urge for murder took hold of him, was responsible for the deaths of at least nine people in the 1920s. He mutilated their bodies with knives, scissors, or hammers.

Kurten was, by today's standards, a classic example of an organized killer. He had grown up in an abusive home and had a history of animal abuse, arson, and burglary. While serving jail time for the latter crime, he heard about and became fascinated with the unsolved case of London's infamous Jack the Ripper.

Kurten was a smooth talker and a good actor who lured his victims to horrible deaths with his outwardly friendly appearance. His neighbors, says author Brian Innes, in his book *Serial Killers*, "described him as a mild, conservative, soft-spoken man, a churchgoer, and a lover of young children."[56] Kurten was even married during his bloody killing spree.

Although Kurten's murders occurred long before professional profilers existed, his case reveals important things about the process of modern profiling.

First, in the midst of his career as a killer, Kurten felt compelled to write to the very people who were desperately trying to catch him. To the local newspaper, he sent maps to the bodies of two of his victims, and to the police, he sent anonymous letters—inspired, perhaps, by the work of Jack the Ripper, whom Kurten greatly admired.

A second important profiling trait was that after his capture, Kurten was clearly willing to talk about why he had done what he did. Before he could go into greater detail, he was beheaded, which was the penalty in those days for murder in Germany.

German murderer Peter Kurten murdered at least nine people in the 1920s. Profilers didn't exist during this time, but his case exhibits important things about the process of modern profiling.

Conversing with known serial criminals, both during their crime sprees (if they communicate with police) and then after their arrest (usually as they sit in prison serving life terms or waiting for the death penalty), is one of a profiler's most important jobs.

It is how profilers get deep into the minds of serial offenders, learning what makes them tick so they can recognize the kinds of traits and behaviors that will help them track down other killers.

By the Numbers

59%

Percentage of Americans who believe that racial profiling is widespread.

Prison Interviews

"What causes a suspect to confess?" ask FBI profiler Russell Vorpagel and and author Joseph Harrington. "Why do some suspects have a need to be caught? Why do others meticulously hide their crimes? And still others have a need to toy with the police?"[57] Vorpagel and Harrington say good investigators train themselves to think like a criminal. "Many criminals have told [profilers] their fantasies," they explain. "This is part of profiling."[58]

Prison, in fact, was where modern profiling really took root. The first profilers officially assigned by the FBI to use psychology as a tool for tracking down offenders spent most of their time in prisons in the beginning of their career. They needed to compile case studies of serial criminals. Profiling, after all, involves inductive reasoning, or looking at details in a new case that are similar to cases the profiler has seen before.

As one of those original FBI profilers, John Douglas writes, with coauthor Mark Olshaker, about the time he spent in prisons in his book *Mindhunter*. "The prison visits became a regular practice," Douglas says. "Wherever I found myself, I'd find out what prison or penitentiary was nearby and who of interest was 'in residence.'"[59] His interviews numbered in the dozens, and they gave Douglas and his fellow profilers a stronger basis for the job they were doing.

A scene from the film Silence of the Lambs *(1991), shows Clarice Starling (Jodie Foster) trying to get into the mind of serial killer Hannibal Lecter (Anthony Hopkins).*

"The more of these interviews I did, the more confident I began to feel," he says. "Everything had to be interpreted through hard work and extensive review on our part. What the interviews were doing, though, was letting us see the way the offender's mind worked, getting a feel for them, allowing us to start walking in their shoes."[60]

Conducting an Interview

In the decades since Douglas spent so much time conducting those early interviews, profiling has come a long way. More and more often, interviews are used not just to study criminals who have already been caught but to narrow down suspect lists in unsolved crimes and help police conduct the kinds of suspect interviews that will hopefully lead to a confession.

Written Evidence

A ransom note. A tablet of lined paper with a page of "practice" writing. A felt-tip pen used to write the ransom note found in a kitchen container.

These items are some of the evidence profilers examined from the murder scene of child beauty queen JonBenet Ramsey on December 26, 1996.

The note, and the "practice" draft, became the details on which much of the investigation focused. Profilers examined the note to make predictions about its author. The writer is a white male in his thirties or forties, read the profile. He probably has a business background and he is almost certainly familiar with the Ramsey family.

A forty-one-year-old white teacher named John Mark Karr confessed to JonBenet's murder in 2006. He did not exactly match the profile. His confession was later revealed to be a hoax.

Is the profile of JonBenet's killer accurate? Police still do not know. As is always the case in profiling, the accuracy of a profile can only be judged when the case is solved. JonBenet's killer has not yet been found.

In 2006, John Mark Karr (center) is led to a news conference after his arrest in Thailand in connection with the 1996 murder of 6-year-old JonBenet Ramsey in Boulder, Colorado.

Serial killer Jeffrey Dahmer (left foreground) is pictured during court proceedings in 1991. Profilers also assist lawyers with potential questions to ask in court and help them decide which witnesses to put on the stand.

The profile of a serial criminal usually contains many details about the person's probable personality. Interrogations of suspects should be performed in a way that is most likely to make a guilty person confess. A profiler, by looking at what the offender has done in a particular case, will be able to tell police if this is an organized or a disorganized person, as well as some of the things that are important to him or her. A profiler can tell police what kinds of questions to ask during the interrogation, as well as what time of day a confession would be most likely to come, in what kind of room, and with what kinds of "props" on the table, such as photos or souvenirs from the crime scenes.

If and when an offender is arrested and a case goes to trial, profilers sometimes also help lawyers decide the best kind of questions to ask and the best witnesses to put on the stand. FBI profiler Robert K. Ressler himself was asked to testify in the case of Jeffrey Dahmer, who was on trial for killing at least seventeen people. Surprisingly, Ressler was a defense witness who supported the defense's argument that Dahmer was insane. Dahmer was widely considered to be an organized killer—the kind usually deemed as sane in a criminal trial. Ressler had concluded that Dahmer, at times, was disorganized in his murders. Ressler's testimony was intended to make the insanity defense more believable to the jury.

"The idea of 'Ressler for the defense' raised eyebrows," Ressler said. "But I did believe that my expertise could contribute to an understanding of the man and his crimes that would provide the necessary basis for a fair adjudication [judgment] of the case."[61]

Communication with the killers—whether during trial, in a prison interview, or by letters sent to the police or the media—is becoming ever more important to the process of criminal profiling. It has to be, because some offenders put communication at the very center of their crimes.

Criminal Correspondence

"This is the Zodiac speaking."[62] So began a note mailed in 1969 to the *San Francisco Chronicle*, one of that city's major newspapers. The editors knew they were hearing from the Zodiac Killer again. His was one of the most frightening killing sprees on record, in part because the deaths were followed by letters—sloppy and poorly written, but dropping enough clues about the crimes to confirm that they did, indeed, come from the killer's own hand.

Like another killer from a century before who signed one of his own notes to the press with "Better known as Jack the ripper," the Zodiac recorded his killings with a string of letters. His were signed with a mysterious symbol, a cross over a circle. The symbol, interpreted as a sign of the zodiac, earned the killer a nickname he liked so much that he adopted it in his future letters, much like Jack the Ripper did with his own name. Also like Jack the Ripper, the Zodiac was never caught.

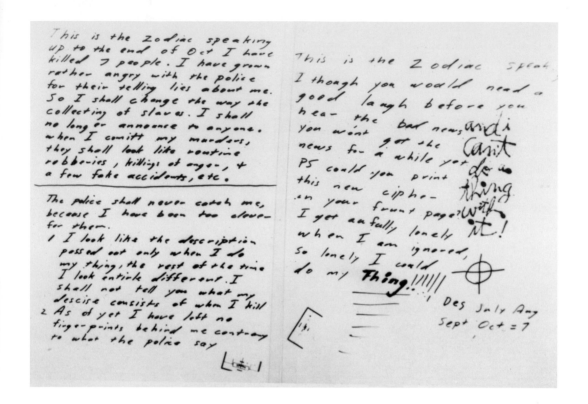

A note written by the Zodiac killer begins with words that terrified the San Francisco bay area in 1969: "This is the Zodiac speaking."

Both of these cases illustrate the perverse need of some killers to communicate with police and the media. Often, like both the Ripper and the Zodiac, they taunt police with phrases, such as Jack's famous line, "Catch me if you can," and their letters usually hold the frightening promise of more violence to come. For profilers, communication like this can both help and harm a case.

It is helpful because it is a strong behavioral clue. The need to communicate tells profilers volumes about a criminal's frame of mind and why he feels the need to broadcast his crimes. Is he playing a game or is he after fame?

Correspondence can also make profiling much more challenging, however, especially because of copycats, people who also write letters pretending to be the killer. Then profilers have the added challenge of deciding which letters are really from the killer and which might be fakes. In the case of the Zodiac, investigators knew the killer's letters were authentic because he discussed crime details that police had not released, details only the person who committed the murders could have known.

The author of Jack the Ripper's letters was not always so obvious. In fact, some modern investigators looking back on the evidence from that case suspect that the first letters might not have been written by the killer at all, and that his jealousy that someone else was taking credit for his work made him respond with his own letters to the police.

"When I first began to go through the Ripper letters," says author Patricia Cornwell in her book *Portrait of a Killer: Jack the Ripper Case Closed*, "I concurred with what police and most people believe: Almost all of the letters are hoaxes or the communications of mentally unbalanced people."[63] Although Cornwell goes on to say that after further study, she began to suspect that Jack the Ripper had, in fact, written most of the letters himself, her uncertainty on the matter shows just how confusing written correspondence from a criminal can be.

There are other challenges of profiling a criminal's correspondence. For example, a letter filled with misspelled words and mistakes in grammar does not always mean that its author is uneducated. A profiler might be able to determine that the words have been spelled wrong on purpose to make police believe that the criminal is stupid or comes from another country.

Such a letter might be designed to throw investigators off the trail, but it may in fact lead a profiler in a whole different direction. To the profiler, such a letter could point to a very educated person, perhaps even one who speaks several languages. So the offender's efforts might backfire, perhaps helping profilers narrow down the suspect list to highly educated people.

All correspondence that criminals have with police can help solve a case. But sometimes, letters are the entire key to preventing a murder from happening in the first place. These cases are kidnappings for ransom, and a profiler's skills at reading not just the ransom note but the person who wrote it can be the only hope of bringing the victim home alive.

Kidnappers, Ransom Notes, and the Criminal Profiler

In 1927 Charles Lindbergh, a handsome, former U.S. Army pilot, succeeded at something no other living person had done. He flew over the Atlantic Ocean alone in an airplane, and the feat made him one of the most famous and wealthy people in the United States.

When Lindbergh's first child was born, the country was in the midst of the Great Depression. People were starving, and kidnapping for ransom had become a popular crime. One night in 1932, when Lindbergh's son was just twenty months old, he disappeared from his nursery and was never seen alive again.

The search for the kidnapper was the biggest, most publicized case of its day. Every newspaper in the country followed the investigation. There were plenty of theories, and many fingers were pointed at Mafia gangsters. A respected psychiatrist named Dudley Shoenfeld took one look at the ransom notes the kidnapper was writing and came to a very different conclusion.

The notes appeared to be written by someone with very poor spelling and terrible grammar. The first note, which the kidnapper left in the nursery in place of the baby he had taken, read, "We warn you for making anyding public or for notify the Police." It further stated that the child was in "gut" (not "good") care.[64]

"To an untrained observer," says Lloyd C. Gardner, author of *The Case That Never Dies: The Lindbergh Kidnapping*, "it might appear to be poor English grammar."[65] To Shoenfeld, however, the notes appeared to have been written by someone whose first language was not English. It was determined by translators that the notes were grammatically correct once they

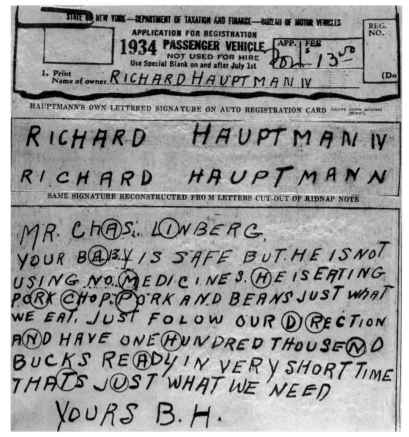

STATE OF NEW YORK—DEPARTMENT OF TAXATION AND FINANCE—BUREAU OF MOTOR VEHICLES

REG. NO.

APPLICATION FOR REGISTRATION

1934 PASSENGER VEHICLE

NOT USED FOR HIRE
Use Special Blank on and after July 1st

APP. FEB

1. Print
Name of owner: RICHARD HAUPTMAN IV

(Do

HAUPTMANN'S OWN LETTERED SIGNATURE ON AUTO REGISTRATION CARD (shown above, enlarged below).

RICHARD HAUPTMAN IV

RICHARD HAUPTMANN

SAME SIGNATURE RECONSTRUCTED FROM LETTERS CUT OUT OF KIDNAP NOTE

MR. CHAS. LINBERG,
YOUR BABY IS SAFE BUT HE IS NOT
USING NO MEDICINES. HE IS EATING
PORK CHOP. PORK AND BEANS JUST WHAT
WE EAT. JUST FOLOW OUR DIRECTION
AND HAVE ONE HUNDRED THOUSEND
BUCKS READY IN VERY SHORT TIME
THATS JUST WHAT WE NEED
YOURS B.H.

Three writing samples compare the writing of Bruno Hauptmann (the top two samples) with the Lindbergh kidnapping ransom note, and were instrumental in Hauptmann being convicted of the murder of the Lindbergh baby.

were translated into German, and Shoenfeld advised police that they should be looking for a German.

Shoenfeld stayed with the case until the end, providing what was, at the time, an early example of profiling. He predicted that the kidnapper was a fully functional, law-abiding member of society, but one who had schizophrenia. He insisted that the kidnapper acted alone, not as part of a gang.

When German-born Bruno Richard Hauptmann was arrested and put on trial for the crime, Shoenfeld still acted the part of the profiler in a time when no such profession existed. He attended the trial, dropping hints to prosecutors about how to question Hauptmann on the stand.

In the hopes of gathering data, Shoenfeld asked that Hauptmann "be kept alive to serve as a subject in the study

Should Profilers Testify in Criminal Trials?

Criminal profiles involve a lot of guesswork, and for that reason they are typically not used by prosecutors in criminal trials. A profile might indeed lead police to the right suspect, but then it is up to police to establish the trail of hard evidence linking that person to the crime.

In a few cases, however, a profile has become part of that trail of hard evidence. In one case in Delaware in 1989, a profile helped police track down the killer of two young women because it described an offender who would drive a van with high mileage and who would find his victims by cruising the streets. A female officer was assigned to work undercover to bait the offender. A man who fit the profile did indeed pick her up. Carpet fibers from his van matched those found on the two victims, and police arrested the driver.

The court admitted the profile as evidence at the trial, deciding that a criminal profile creates probable cause to search a suspect's belongings.

of the criminal mind."[66] Shoenfeld's hopes were dashed when Hauptmann was convicted and put to death for the kidnapping and murder of baby Lindbergh. But the psychiatrist made history by profiling Hauptmann's characteristics from his written communication, and he helped establish the modern role of the profiler, not just in tracking down an offender but in assisting at trials and studying convicts to learn about the workings of a criminal mind.

Shoenfeld's theories about the identity of the kidnapper also pointed to one of the great controversies of profiling. To say that the killer of America's most famous baby was a German, at a time when most Americans had a low opinion of Germany because it was a U.S. enemy during World War I, could have been considered a prejudiced assessment. The profiling process has always been criticized for potentially reflecting the profiler's own beliefs and stereotypes.

Profiling, Past and Future

Profiling has been compared to witchcraft and called hocus-pocus. It has been so eerily accurate that police investigators in some cases have suspected a psychic influence was at work, and it has also been so widely off base that critics say it should never be used again.

Criminal profiling has always perched on the fence between proven investigative methods and wild guessing with the hope of being right at least some of the time. In difficult cases, however, when police departments are faced with the kinds of crimes that they are certain will happen again, even a seemingly wild guess that points them in a new direction can be welcome help.

Criminal profilers are quick to point out that they perform just one part of an active investigation and are just one member of a crime-busting team. "We do not catch criminals. Local police catch criminals," Douglas says. "What we try to do is *assist* local police in focusing their investigations, then suggest some proactive techniques that might help draw a criminal out." Once a suspect is tracked down, he says, "we will try to formulate a strategy to bring out the defendant's true personality during the trial."[67]

Once a criminal is caught, the profile is not used again. Rarely, if ever, is a profile allowed to be used as evidence in a trial. This is partly because profiles are just guesses, and good defense attorneys would make sure a jury understands that police were guessing. Another reason profiles are poor evidence in trials is their reputation for stereotyping people, as was possibly true in the Lindbergh kidnapping profile. Any profile, after all, is based at least in part on stereotypes, because it depends on the profiler's knowledge of other people who have done similar things. A profiler makes assumptions, usually negative ones, about the offender's character, and courts almost always

Bruno Richard Hauptmann, convicted of the Lindbergh baby kidnapping and murder, poses for his mug shot in 1934. Stereotyping may have played a part in Hauptmann's conviction, since many Americans had a low opinion of both Germans and Germany at the time.

see profiles as pictures of prejudice, especially if the profile and not hard evidence led to a suspect's arrest.

"Judicial use of criminal profiling has a poor track record,"[68] says Scott Ingram, author of the article, "If the Profile Fits: Admitting Criminal Psychological Profiles into Evidence in Criminal Trials." He notes that trials in which profiles were admitted as evidence have resulted in convictions that were later overturned.

"Nonetheless," Ingram says, "criminal psychological profiles should be admitted as evidence in criminal trials." He describes them as "both relevant and reliable in that they have a basis in established psychological and sociological principles."[69]

Clearly, it is the scientific side of profiling that gives it credibility. To the extent that profiles are based on inductive reasoning, or scientific statistics from past cases, profiling could be called a scientific process.

If that is true, some people believe that computers and databases could one day take the place of a criminal profiler. Profilers themselves believe otherwise. "There are many reasons that computers cannot be profilers," says author Deborah Schurman-Kauflin. "So much of profiling involves not only insight into physical evidence but intuition as well. . . . This is not to say that profiling involves psychic phenomenon. It simply means that a person is a better judge of human character than a computer."[70]

For Douglas, profiling is about more than just crunching data. A computer, he says, does not do the most important part of profiling: walking in the shoes of the offender and the victim. "The fact of the matter is that while we use computers a lot in our work and they are capable of some impressive things," he says, "some other more complex things they simply can't do and may never be able to do. Profiling is like writing. You can give a computer all the rules of grammar and syntax and style, but it still can't write the book."[71]

Although the process of profiling has its opponents, most law experts agree that when violent serial killers, rapists, bombers, arsonists, and other dangerous people are on the loose, investigators have a responsibility to combine forces and use every possible tool at their disposal to save lives and put an end to the terror.

Criminal profiles may not always be perfect, but they have helped put an end to the carnage of such killers as the Mad Bomber, the Sacramento Vampire, and the Railway Killer.

The more criminals who are captured, the more deviant minds profilers will have to study, and the better they will become at what they do: stopping the most dangerous criminal offenders before they can strike again.

Notes

Introduction: Profiling Criminals and Their Crimes

1. Arthur Conan Doyle, "A Case of Identity," in *Sherlock Holmes: The Major Stories with Contemporary Critical Essays*, ed. John A. Hodgson. New York: St. Martin's, 1994, p. 88.

2. Doyle, "A Case of Identity," p. 82.

Chapter One: What Profilers Do

3. Gregg O. McCrary, *The Unknown Darkness: Profiling the Predators Among Us*. New York: HarperCollins, 2003, p. 9.

4. McCrary, *The Unknown Darkness*, p. 10.

5. McCrary, *The Unknown Darkness*, p. 26.

6. McCrary, *The Unknown Darkness*, p. 21.

7. John E. Douglas, Robert K. Ressler, Ann W. Burgess, and Carol R. Hartman, "Criminal Profiling from Crime Scene Analysis," in *Profilers: Leading Investigators Take You Inside the Criminal Mind*, eds. John H. Campbell and Don DeNevi. New York: Prometheus, 2004, p. 17.

8. Deborah Schurman-Kauflin, *The New Predator: Women Who Kill. Profiles of Female Serial Killers*. New York: Algora, 2000, pp. 179, 197.

9. Douglas et al., "Criminal Profiling," p. 17.

10. Schurman-Kauflin, *The New Predator*, p. 217.

11. Katherine Ramsland, "Criminal Profiling Part I. History and Method: Criminal Analysis," truTV Crime Library: Criminal Minds and Methods. www.crimelibrary.com/criminal_mind/profiling/history_method/index.html.

12. Ramsland, "Criminal Profiling Part I."

13. McCrary, *The Unknown Darkness*, p. 10.

14. Mary Ellen O'Toole, "Criminal Profiling: The FBI Uses Criminal Investigative Analysis to Solve Crimes," in *Profilers: Leading Investigators Take You Inside the Criminal Mind*, eds. Campbell and DeNevi, p. 225.

15. Ramsland, "Criminal Profiling Part I."

16. Douglas et al., "Criminal Profiling," pp. 17–18.

17. Douglas et al., "Criminal Profiling," p. 19.

18. Douglas et al., "Criminal Profiling," p. 27.

19. D. Kim Rossmo, "Geographic Profiling Update," in *Profilers: Leading Investigators Take You Inside the Criminal Mind*, eds. Campbell and DeNevi, p. 294.

Chapter Two: Profiling the Crime Scene

20. Quoted in Ramsland, "Criminal Profiling Part I."

21. Rossmo, "Geographic Profiling Update," p. 298.

22. Russell Vorpagel and Joseph Harrington, *Profiles in Murder: An FBI Legend Dissects Killers and Their Crimes*. New York: Plenum, 1998, p. 47.

23. Vorpagel and Harrington, *Profiles in Murder*, p. 49.

24. Schurman-Kauflin, *The New Predator*, pp. 141–142.

25. Robert K. Ressler and Ann W. Burgess, "Classifying Sexual Homicide Crime Scenes: Interrater Reliability," in *Profilers: Leading Investigators Take You Inside the Criminal Mind*, eds. Campbell and DeNevi, p. 95.

26. Brent Turvey, *Criminal Profiling: An Introduction to Behavioral Evidence Analysis*, 2nd ed. San Diego, CA: Academic Press, 2002, p. 230.

27. Turvey, *Criminal Profiling*, pp. 280, 282.

28. John Douglas, with Mark Olshaker, *Mindhunter*. New York: Scribner, 1995, p. 252.

29. Rossmo, "Geographic Profiling Update," p. 299.

Chapter Three: Profiling the Victim

30. Michael R. King, "A Multidisciplinary Approach to Solving Cold Cases," in *Profilers: Leading Investigators Take You Inside the Criminal Mind*, eds. Campbell and DeNevi, p. 260.

31. Douglas et al., "Criminal Profiling," p. 15.

32. O'Toole, "Criminal Profiling," p. 226.

33. O'Toole, "Criminal Profiling," p. 226.

34. Brent Turvey, "Victimology," truTV Crime Library: Criminal Minds and Methods. www.crimelibrary.com/criminal_mind/profiling/victimology/2.html.

35. King, "A Multidisciplinary Approach," p. 261.

36. O'Toole, "Criminal Profiling," p. 227.

37. Richard N. Kocsis, *Criminal Profiling: Principles and Practice*. Totowa, NJ: Humana, 2006, p. 78.

38. O'Toole, "Criminal Profiling," p. 227.

39. Quoted in Brian Innes, *Serial Killers*. London: Quercus, 2007, p. 38.

Chapter Four: Profiling the Offender

40. Robert J. Hormant and Daniel B. Kennedy, "Psychological Aspects of Crime Scene Profiling," in *Current Perspectives in Forensic Psychology and Criminal Justice*, eds. Curt R. Bartoli and Anne M. Bartoli. Thousand Oaks, CA: Sage, 2005, p. 52.

41. Brent Turvey, *Deductive Criminal Profiling: Comparing Applied Methodologies Between Inductive and Deductive Criminal Profiling Techniques*. Knowledge Solutions

Library, 1998. www.corpus-delicti.com/
Profiling_law.html.

42. Turvey, *Deductive Criminal Profiling*.

43. Douglas et al., "Criminal Profiling,"
pp. 17, 26.

44. Douglas, with Olshaker, *Mindhunter*,
p. 178.

45. Robert K. Ressler, "How to Interview
a Cannibal," in *Profilers: Leading
Investigators Take You Inside the Criminal
Mind*, eds. Campbell and DeNevi,
p. 138.

46. Ressler, "How to Interview a Cannibal,"
p. 138.

47. Colin Evans, *The Casebook of Forensic
Detection: How Science Solved 100 of the
World's Most Baffling Crimes*. New York:
Wiley, 1996, p. 165.

48. Evans, *The Casebook of Forensic Detection*,
p. 65.

49. Stephen Labaton, "Portrait of a Serial
Bomber Emerges After Parcel Blasts,"
New York Times, June 26, 1993. http://
query.nytimes.com/gst/fullpage.html?
res=9F0CE1D81030F935A15755C0A
965958260&sec=&spon=&pagewante
d=2.

50. Douglas, with Olshaker, *Mindhunter*,
p. 327.

51. Quoted in Del Quentin Wilber, "Man
Arrested in D.C. Area's Arson Wave,"
Washington Post, April 28, 2005. www.
washingtonpost.com/wp-dyn/content/
article/2005/04/27/AR2005042700599.
html.

52. Mary Mavromatis, "Serial Arson:
Repetitive Firesetting and Pyromania,"
in *Serial Offenders: Current Thought, Recent
Findings*, ed. Louis B. Schlesinger. Boca
Raton, FL: CRC, 2000, p. 68.

53. Schurman-Kauflin, *The New Predator*, p.
18.

54. Schurman-Kauflin, *The New Predator*, pp.
181, 217.

55. Schurman-Kauflin, *The New Predator*, p.
179.

Chapter Five: Criminal Communication in Profiling

56. Innes, *Serial Killers*, p. 36.

57. Vorpagel and Harrington, *Profiles in
Murder*, p. 113.

58. Vorpagel and Harrington, *Profiles in
Murder*, p. 114.

59. Douglas, with Olshaker, *Mindhunter*,
p. 116.

60. Douglas, with Olshaker, *Mindhunter*,
p. 117.

61. Ressler, "How to Interview a Cannibal,"
p. 146.

62. Innes, *Serial Killers*, p. 83.

63. Patricia Cornwell, *Portrait of a Killer: Jack
the Ripper Case Closed*. New York: Berkley,
2002, p. 50.

64. Quoted in Lloyd C. Gardner, *The Case
That Never Dies: The Lindbergh Kidnapping*.
Piscataway, NJ: Rutgers University Press,
2004, p. 129.

65. Gardner, *The Case That Never Dies*, p. 129.

66. Quoted in Gardner, *The Case That Never Dies*, p. 363.

67. Douglas, with Olshaker, *Mindhunter*, p. 31.

68. Scott Ingram, "If the Profile Fits: Admitting Criminal Psychological Profiles into Evidence in Criminal Trials," *Journal of Urban and Contemporary Law* 54, 1998, pp. 239–267, 249.

69. Ingram, "If the Profile Fits," p. 267.

70. Schurman-Kauflin, *The New Predator*, p. 219.

71. Douglas, with Olshaker, *Mindhunter*, p. 151.

Glossary

arson: The criminal act of setting fire to property.

criminal profiling: The process of making assumptions about a crime or criminal based on characteristics of the crime.

deductive reasoning: Using a general conclusion about something to make guesses about specific details.

disorganized crime scene: A crime scene that reveals little evidence of preplanning or attempts by the criminal to avoid detection.

geographic profiling: Analysis of the locations and times at which a crime takes place, used to draw conclusions about the offender.

high-risk victim: A crime victim who often spent time in dangerous situations.

hypothesis: An assumption about something, based on facts or evidence.

inductive reasoning: Using specific details about something to draw a general conclusion.

inference: A guess.

interrogation: The act of questioning someone, usually a suspect, in a criminal case.

low-risk victim: A crime victim who rarely or never spent time in dangerous situations.

medium-risk victim: A crime victim who occasionally spent time in dangerous situations.

modus operandi: The method a person uses to conduct a crime.

motive: The reason a person commits a crime.

organized crime scene: A crime scene that reveals evidence of preplanning and attempts by the criminal to avoid detection.

ransom: Money paid for the release of a person who is held captive.

signature: An action by a criminal during a crime that satisfies psychological or emotional needs of the criminal.

staging: The act of making a crime look as though it occurred differently.

victimology: The study of behaviors and characteristics of crime victims.

For More Information

Books

D.B. Beres, *Killer at Large: Criminal Profilers and the Cases They Solve!* Scholastic, 2006. The science of criminal profiling is described with support from case studies on the Mad Bomber and others. One chapter is devoted to the career path of criminal profilers.

Joan Esherick, *Criminal Psychology and Personality Profiling*. Mason Crest, 2005. Case studies of actual crimes are used to explain a profiler's various roles in crime investigations and courts of law, as well as hazards and challenges of the job.

Barbara R. Kirwin, *The Mad, the Bad and the Innocent: The Criminal Mind on Trial—Tales of a Forensic Psychologist*. Little, Brown, 1997. A forensic psychologist relates the details of infamous killers and her quest to understand their minds.

Newspaper Articles

Leon Fooksman and Jerome Burdi, "Profilers Point to One Killer in Three Boca Murders," *South Florida Sun-Sentinel*, February 8, 2008. www.sun-sentinel.com/news/local/sfl-flp-profilers0208pnfeb08,0,7776101.story?track=rss.

Kim Janssen, "Profiler: 'He's Still Very Dangerous,'" *Chicago Sun-Times*, February 7, 2008. www.suntimes.com/news/metro/782275,profile020708.article. Former FBI profilers Gregg O. McCrary and Clint Van Zandt profile the gunman who murdered five women in a Chicago clothing store on February 2, 2008.

Film

Serial Killers: Profiling the Criminal Mind, A&E Home Video, 2000. 200 minutes. FBI criminal profiler John Douglas leads a journey through the world of criminal profiling and discusses famous murderers, such as Charles Manson and John Wayne Gacy.

Web Sites

Deviant Crimes (www.deviantcrimes.com). In-depth discussions of psychopathic criminals, crimes, and forensic investigations are presented on this site. Sections on profiling and victimology give a good overview of both topics.

John Douglas Mindhunter.com (www.johndouglasmindhunter.com). John Douglas, chief of the FBI's Investigative Support Unit and a bestselling author of books on criminal profiling, hosts this Web site with links to articles, books, frequently asked questions, and an e-mail newsletter.

Swiss Criminal Profiling Scientific Research Site (www.criminalprofiling. ch). History, theories, and applications of criminal profiling are discussed on this site, as well as case studies. Many resources are offered for further research.

truTV Crime Library: Profiling Interactive (www.crimelibrary.com/criminal_mind/ profiling/profiling_2/index.html). Try your hand at being a profiler. Read the clues in a murder case and decide what to do next—then learn why your decisions are right or wrong.

Index

Picture Credits

Cover: © Corbis/SuperStock

© Alen MacWeeney/Corbis, 32

Alex Wong/Getty Images, 34

AP Images, 11, 19, 21, 23, 27, 39, 40, 44, 45, 50, 52, 56, 59, 64, 69, 71, 73, 79, 80, 88

© Bettmann/Corbis, 82, 85

Elaine Thompson-Pool/Getty Images, 36

Evening Standard/Hulton Archive/Getty Images, 66

Imagno/Hulton Archive/Getty Images, 76

Lambert/Getty Images, 9

Library of Congress, 17

Mario Ruiz/Time & Life Pictures/Getty Images, 61

Mark Wilson/Getty Images, 14

Orion/The Kobal Collection/Regan, Ken, 78

Paul Harris/Getty Images, 30

Peter Stackpole/Time & Life Pictures/Getty Images, 13

About the Author

Jenny MacKay lives in Sparks, Nevada, with her husband, Andy, and their children, Ryan and Natalie. MacKay is a science, technical, and medical editor and has written for many newspapers and magazines. Every week, she watches *Forensic Fridays* on Court TV.